Lecture Notes in Artificial Intelligence 13743

Subseries of Lecture Notes in Computer Science

More information about this subseries at https://link.springer.com/bookseries/1244

Fabian Lorig · Emma Norling (Eds.)

Multi-Agent-Based Simulation XXIII

23rd International Workshop, MABS 2022
Virtual Event, May 8–9, 2022
Revised Selected Papers

 Springer

Editors
Fabian Lorig 🆔
Malmö University
Malmö, Sweden

Emma Norling 🆔
University of Sheffield
Sheffield, UK

ISSN 0302-9743   ISSN 1611-3349 (electronic)
Lecture Notes in Artificial Intelligence
ISBN 978-3-031-22946-6   ISBN 978-3-031-22947-3 (eBook)
https://doi.org/10.1007/978-3-031-22947-3

LNCS Sublibrary: SL7 – Artificial Intelligence

This Springer imprint is published by the registered company Springer Nature Switzerland AG
The registered company address is: Gewerbestrasse 11, 6330 Cham, Switzerland

Preface

This volume presents revised papers from the 23rd International Workshop on Multi-Agent-Based Simulation (MABS 2022), a two-day workshop collocated with the International Conference on Autonomous Agents and Multi-Agent Systems (AAMAS 2022). The workshop was originally planned to be held in Auckland, New Zealand, but due to COVID-19 related travel restrictions and for reasons of precaution, the event took place virtually during May 8–9, 2022.

The meeting of researchers from Multi-Agent Systems (MAS) engineering and researchers from the social, economic, and organisational sciences is extensively recognised for its role in cross-fertilisation. It has undoubtedly been an important source of inspiration for the body of knowledge that has been produced in the area. The MABS workshop series continues with its goal to bring together researchers interested in MAS engineering with researchers focused on finding efficient solutions to model complex social systems, in areas such as economics, management, and organisational and social sciences in general. More information about the MABS workshop series may be found at https://www.pcs.usp.br/~mabs/.

The workshop provides a forum for social scientists, MAS and AI researchers and developers, and simulation researchers to assess the current state of the art in the modelling and simulation of social systems and MAS, to identify where existing approaches can be successfully applied, to learn about new approaches and explore future research challenges, and to exchange ideas and knowledge in an inter-disciplinary environment.

This year's workshop was opened by a special session on "Simulations related to the crisis". A keynote talk on "Cognitive agents for policy making in the covid crisis?" was given by Frank Dignum from Umeå University, Sweden. The workshop was concluded with a panel discussion focusing on the topics of MABS 2022 as well as on hot topics and current challenges to be addressed in future editions of MABS.

For MABS 2022, 17 submissions were received and reviewed by at least three members of the Program Committee in a single-blind review process. Based on the provided reviews, the Program Chairs selected 11 submissions for presentation. After the workshop, the authors of these papers were invited to prepare a revised extended version of their manuscript, taking ideas, feedback, and discussions from the workshop into account. The revised articles were once again reviewed by the Program Chairs, to ensure the high quality of the published papers.

We are very grateful to all authors, presenters, members of the Program Committee, and all participants taking part in the discussions for their contribution to MABS 2022.

May 2022

Fabian Lorig
Emma Norling

Organization

Program Chairs

Fabian Lorig   Malmö University, Sweden
Emma Norling   University of Sheffield, UK

MABS Steering Committee

Frédéric Amblard   University of Toulouse, France
Luis Antunes   University of Lisbon, Portugal
Paul Davidsson   Malmö University, Sweden
Emma Norling   University of Sheffield, UK
Mario Paolucci   National Research Council, Italy
Jaime Simão Sichman   University of São Paulo, Brazil
Samarth Swarup   University of Virginia, USA
Takao Terano   Tokyo Institute of Technology, Japan
Harko Verhagen   Stockholm University, Sweden

Program Committee

Diana Francisca Adamatti   Federal University of Rio Grande, Brazil
Shah Jamal Alam   Habib University, Pakistan
Fred Amblard   Toulouse 1 Capitole University, France
João Balsa   University of Lisbon, Portugal
Johan Barthelemy   University of Wollongong, Australia
Sung-Bae Cho   Yonsei University, South Korea
Paul Davidsson   Malmö University, Sweden
Frank Dignum   Umeå University, Sweden
Bruce Edmonds   Manchester Metropolitan University, UK
Benoit Gaudou   University of Toulouse, France
Nick Gotts   Independent Researcher, UK
Rainer Hegselmann   Bayreuth University, Germany
Wander Jager   University of Groningen, The Netherlands
Bill Kennedy   George Mason University, USA
Ruth Meyer   Centre for Policy Modelling, UK
Jean-Pierre Muller   CIRAD, France
John Murphy   Argonne National Laboratory, USA
Luis Gustavo Nardin   École des Mines de Saint-Étienne, France

Contents

Land Use Management Using Multi-Agent Based Simulation in a Watershed in South of the Brazil

Bruna da Silva Leitzke$^{(\boxtimes)}$ ⓘ and Diana Francisca Adamatti ⓘ

Center for Computational Sciences, Federal University of Rio Grande,
Rio Grande 96203-900, Brazil
brunaleitzke@hotmail.com

Abstract. The change in land use in a region can have huge impacts on the environment. For land use management to be effective, it is necessary to explore the region of interest, its behavior, and the impact of each change. This study aims to present the development and simulation of an agent-based model for land use management in the Arroio Fragata Watershed, located in the south of Brazil. For this, regional data, maps of land use, and maps of sub-watersheds were used. And the agents were defined as managers who modify land uses in the region. Through some parameters and variables, a volume of water was defined that varied with each change in land use. The impact on the environment was analysed by varying the number of managers and land uses. The model generated satisfactory results and described the behavior of the agents and the environment according to the defined rules. It became conspicuous that some land uses to generate a greater impact, depending on the water consumption and the area of occupation in the region. In addition, some simulations showed that despite being the ones that resulted in the greatest changes in the environment, they were not the ones that generated the greatest impact.

Keywords: Land use management · Watershed · Multi-agent system

1 Introduction

Land use management is the area that aims to organize and to plan the implementation of land occupation changes. Changes in land use induced by human actions have been seriously interfering with the environment, reflecting on the well-being of living beings and on the economy [5]. In addition, in watersheds, poor management of land use impacts the amount and quality of water resources, which are needed to carry out various activities, such as irrigation, public supply, leisure, and others [10].

This research was partly supported by Coordenação de Aperfeiçoamento de Pessoal de Nível Superior and Agência Nacional de Águas (88887.335074/2019-00).

F. Lorig and E. Norling (Eds.): MABS 2022, LNAI 13743, pp. 1–15, 2023.
https://doi.org/10.1007/978-3-031-22947-3_1

Methods such as linear and non-linear programming, genetic optimization algorithm, game-based theory, among others, have been used to determine the ideal land use management in several regions [11]. Multiagent Systems (MAS) are tools that facilitate the construction of models on complex and dynamic environments, where agents perceive the environment and act on it [3]. An agent is an autonomous computational entity that acts from stimuli and sensors [14]. Thus, the decision making and interactions of agents generate changes in the environment, which affect their perceptions and decisions [15]. When computationally simulating a MAS, there is a technique called Multi-Agent-Based Simulation (MABS), which makes it possible to describe the behavior of complex systems with multiple domains [7]. Thus, the behavior of land use change and human interactions in the environment can be simulated [13].

Several works have explored the use of MABS in research on land use management. To simulate land use management in agricultural regions of northeastern France, the authors of [9] developed and simulated an MAS. For it, they defined the agents as managers who opposed among themselves to conquer regions. In the [2], a case study was carried out in a region of Uruguay, to understand and predict the effects of changes in land use. The MABS were used to explore the evolution of the system, where a cost and production relationship on land uses was considered. Other work was carried out in [18], which highlighted the concern of the lack of successors for land use management in Japan. An analytical simulation model based on MAS was built to describe changes in groups and forms of management in the region.

In this work, the development and results of a MABS are presented. The objective was to enable an initial study on land use management in a small watershed, located in southern Brazil. The model presented here was built using the GIS Agent-based Modeling Architecture (GAMA) tool, with available flow data, and maps of land use and sub-watersheds. The environment was discretized into regular cells. And in each cell, the land use and the sub-watershed were identified. From this, the agents defined as *managers*, modified the land use in each cell, in specific sub-watersheds.

To determine the impact of land use changes, some variables and parameters that interfered in the initial water volume of the environment were defined. A water consumption value for each land use was defined and determined in each cell. The model was defined with a monthly time scale, and a water recovery value was defined for each season of the year. In addition, the number of managers varied, as well as the intentions to change land use. Simulations show that water is influenced by land use change, and this causes a dramatic change in water volume.

In the following section, the methodology is addressed, where the study region, the GAMA platform, and the construction of the system are presented. The results and discussion are in Sect. 3, where some scenarios are addressed and analysed. And in Sect. 4, are the final considerations of this study.

2 Methodology

2.1 Study Area

The study region of this work is the Arroio Fragata Watershed (AFW), located in the extreme south of Brazil, with an area of approximately $216km^2$. AFW directly influences the Lagoa Mirim and Canal São Gonçalo Hydrographic Basin, which is a transboundary basin between Brazil and Uruguay. This has huge socioeconomic importance, due to the support of water supply for various activities. In Fig. 1, the AFW is illustrated, as well as its discretization in 39 sub-basins with different colors. The ArcLASH module of the Lavras Simulation of Hydrology model was used to make the spatial discretization of the region [1]. This tool was chosen with the intention of improving the MAS in the future. ArcLASH is an extension of ArcGIS® software, which is an important mapping and data analysis tool. To generate the spatial base through ArcLASH, the following data are needed: Digital Elevation Model (DEM); the soil map; soil attributes; the land use map; land use attributes; the location of the control section; the map of the pluviometric and meteorological monitoring stations; and the injunction to define the drainage network.

In this work, we used the land use map obtained from the *Infraestrutura Nacional de Dados Espaciais* portal, available at [8]. The map is illustrated in Fig. 2, and presents 7 land use classes. The percentage of each use class in relation to AFW is: 50.1% agriculture; 4.5% exposed soil; 3.7% forest; 13.2% native forest; 4.8% native field; 22.9% pasture; and 0.8% water. Thus, agriculture and pasture represent the most predominant classes.

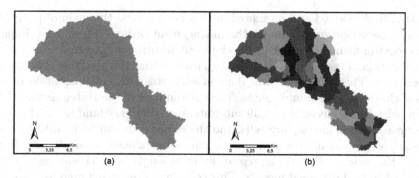

Fig. 1. Arroio Fragata Watershed: (a) region map; and (b) spatial discretization map in sub-watersheds.

2.2 GAMA Platform

In this work, the GAMA tool was chosen for the modeling and simulation development of the MAS. GAMA is a platform based on the Eclipse tool, of which it is an integrated development environment [16]. In addition, it has its own programming language called GAma Modeling Language (GAML), which is coded

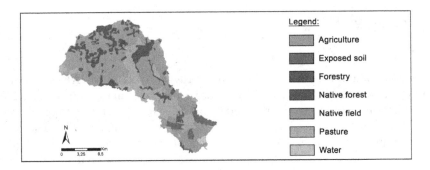

Fig. 2. Arroio Fragata Watershed: land use map.

using the Java computational environment. The platform provides several models, tutorials, and online documentation.

Different types of datasets can be used to build MABS in GAMA, through an integrated development environment. The tool makes it possible to include data from the Geographic Information System, that is, it stores the geometry and attributes of mapped terrestrial data. The simulation environment can be defined in different ways, such as 2D, 3D, or graphical environments. Throughout the simulations, each agent can be inspected, and parameters can be modified. GAMA has been used to model and simulates multi-agent systems in the context of different types of problems, as in the works of [4,6,12,17].

2.3   MABS Development

The MABS, developed and presented in this work, has as the main objective to simulate the actions of agents on the management of land use and the impact on the environment. The MABS development involved verification, calibration and validation. These steps certify and guarantee that the model is close to the expected [3]. The verification was done at each stage of implementation of the rules of the environment and agents. The environment of the system is the AFW region, with its subdivision into 39 sub-watersheds, and the land uses. The environment is divided into square cells, and the dimensions can be modified before the start of the simulation through the parameter *Dimensions_of_the_cells*. However, in this work, cells that represent 300 m in length were chosen, generating a mesh with 2574 occupied meshes. This cell dimension was chosen for two reasons: (i) the database was generated from the DEM with a spacing of $30m$, which was obtained through the U.S. Geological Survey[1]. In this way, for this work, an approximation of the spatial discretization of the data and the MAS environment was sought. (ii) with a grid spacing of 300 m, MABS presented simulations with efficient computational time and processing. This did not occur with smaller dimensions for the cells.

---

[1] https://www.usgs.gov/.

The initial amount of water in the environment was defined as a volume of water (*vol_water*) with a value of 3000 (representing $3000 \times 10^7 L$). This amount was based on flow data, which are available on the Hidroweb[2] portal. From the flow data, the volumetric flow ratio was used to convert the data into volume, and define an initial value for the region. For each land use a water consumption value was defined, except for water land use. In Table 1 are the initial number of cells per land use and the water consumption.

Table 1. Water consumption by land use in each cell.

Land use	Water consumption	Number of cells	Initial total consumption
Agriculture	1.5	1287	1930.5
Exposed soil	1.2	125	150
Forest	1.0	111	111
Native forest	0.5	325	162.5
Native field	0.3	130	39
Pasture	0.8	576	460.8
Water	0	20	0
Total values:	–	2574	2853.8

Figure 3 presents the simulation interface, which has the environment, parameters, 5 managers, and the grid mesh. The agents, called *managers*, can range from 1 to 10, this amount being determined by the parameter *Number_of_managers*. The agents represent institutions or organizations responsible for managing land use. As this is an initial study, it was decided to define a list of sub-basins for each manager, and a land use change attribute called intention. In this way, each manager is responsible for changing land use in certain sub-basins, according to its intentions to change.

The list of sub-basins for each manager is determined in an orderly method. First, the total number of sub-basins (39) is divided by the number of managers, which varies according to the parameter *Number_of_managers*. This result indicates the approximate amount of sub-watershed to each manager. For example, with the 39 sub-watersheds and 5 managers the division results in 4 managers responsible for 8 sub-watersheds, and 1 responsible for 7 sub-watershed. Sub-watersheds and managers are identified by fixed integers. The first sub-watersheds will be linked to the first manager, the following sub-watersheds to the second manager, and so on. Thus, all sub-watersheds will have a responsible manager and may suffer changes in land use. When starting the simulation, the managers are randomly positioned in one of their respective sub-watershed. Managers have two rules, which are "to move" and "to change" land use. Agents can move throughout the AFW, providing access to all of its sub-basins. For that, in GAMA, the wander action (move randomly) is defined, where the variables of speed (equal to 100) and amplitude of vision (45˙) are implemented.

---

[2] https://www.snirh.gov.br/hidroweb/.

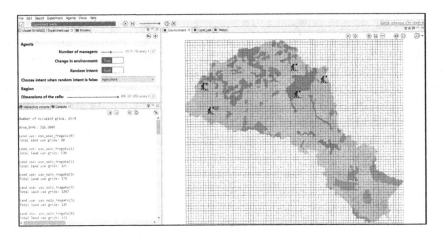

Fig. 3. MAS interface in GAMA.

Land use change can happen in all cells of the AFW. However, agents can modify land use only in their respective sub-watersheds. The intention of each manager is the desirable land use change. From among land uses, the intention is established between agriculture, exposed soil, forest, or pasture. This choice was made with the aim of analysing the impact of land use changes that generate more profitable values in real life. For this reason, the use of native forests, native fields, and water is not defined as the intention.

Each agent modifies the cells altering the land use from the intention. This attribute can be determined randomly or not. For each agent, one of the 4 land uses is defined randomly when the parameter *Random_intent* is true. When false, the intent that will be assigned to all agents is chosen before the simulation. Thus, when moving through the AFW, a manager acts by changing land use in cells that are included in one of its sub-basins, and that have land use different from its intention.

AFW is the environment of the MAS. In it, lists of 39 sub-basins and 7 land uses are determined. In addition, the total water volume and a water recovery rate are defined. In the data instance, there is a volume of water in the environment, calculated from the initial water volume, minus consumption. The time scale is defined as monthly. Thus, when the simulation starts, each cycle is equivalent to one month. Two actions were defined for the environment. Firstly, the water volume is updated in each cycle, from Eq. 1, where n is the reference month, V is the water volume, W is the water consumption sum and S is the water recovery rate.

$$\begin{cases} V_n = V_{n-1} - W_{n-1} + S_n, \\ V_0 = 3000, \quad W_0 = 2853.8. \end{cases} \tag{1}$$

The second action of the environment is to update the season every 3 cyclings and start in summer. Thus, the water recovery rate (S) is updated according to the season, which corresponds to approximately: 2650.99 in summer, 2945.99 in autumn, 3035.99 in winter, and 2785.99 in spring. These parameters were calibrated from tests during the simulations so that the system was stable when there was no change in land use, as illustrated in Fig. 4. To generate this study, the *Change_in_environment* option was inserted which, when false, does not allow agents to modify the environment. This stability does not match reality when there is no change in land use. This analysis was done only to calibrate the water recovery parameters.

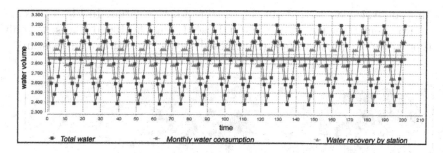

Fig. 4. Monthly amount of water in the environment without change.

In view of the system developed and presented, some scenarios were defined in order to generate discussions and to analyse the MABS. In Table 2, there is a summary of the proposed scenarios when agents modify land use in the environment. For each scenario, 10 simulations were performed, with 10000 cycles (months). This number of cycles was chosen so that it was possible to observe the behavior of the environment with a large change in land use. In addition, it aimed to verify cases of discrepancies in the results, that is when the water volume changes its behavior in terms of its increase or decrease. However, it is understood that this number of cycles cannot be considered realistic considering a monthly timescale. The simulations can be performed with a smaller number of cycles since in most scenarios the environment behavior is between 500 and 1000 cyclings.

Table 2. Determination of parameters for each scenario.

Scenario	Number of managers	Random intent	Intention
1	5	False	Agriculture
2	5	False	Exposed soil
3	5	False	Forest
4	5	False	Pasture
5	2	True	Random
6	5	True	Random
7	10	True	Random

First, the system was analysed when the change occurs for single land use, through 5 managers. In this case, there are 4 scenarios, one for each land use. Subsequently, the intention of the agents was defined as random, and the number of managers varied between 2, 5, and 10. The next section presents some results on the defined scenarios. Each scenario is commented on and verified according to the environment and the graphics generated at the end of the simulations.

3   Results and Discussion

The first analysis was carried out for the first four scenarios. In Fig. 5 presents the environment after the change in land use during the 10000 cycles, for only one type of time (a) agriculture; (b) exposed soil; (c) forest; and (d) pasture.

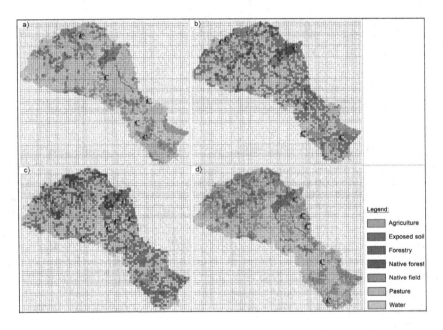

Fig. 5. Environment result for the first four scenarios, with change only to: (a) agriculture; (b) exposed soil; (c) forest; and (d) pasture.

Scenario 1 simulations generated expected results. A significant increase in the demand for water from the environment occurred when the shift was to agriculture. In this case, the simulations generated negative and decreasing water volume. Figure 5(a) shows the AFW map after a change of approximately 510 cells to agriculture, which generated the highest water consumption in the scenario.

The volume of water for scenario 2 was decreasing in all simulations, since exposed soil is the second largest consumer of water in the system. In Fig. 5(b) there is the largest change in the environment for scenario 2, which corresponds to approximately 900 cells altered for exposed soil use. However, this case was not the one that generated greater consumption of water in the environment. Another experiment generated a huge consumption of water. In this case, the change occurred in more cells with uses such as pasture and native forest, which generated a greater and faster demand for water.

In scenario 3, the water volume became positive and increased throughout the simulations. Water consumption in forest use is low when compared to agricultural use, whose region is predominant in the initial environment. Among the four initial scenarios, scenario 3 presented the case with the greatest change in the environment over the 10000 cyclings. The result of this experiment can be seen in Fig. 5(c), with approximately 950 cells with modified land use for the forest. However, this simulation was not the one that generated the lowest water consumption in the scenario.

Scenario 4 also showed an increasing water volume in the simulations. In addition, it generated the highest volumes of water in relation to the other experiments. In Fig. 5(b) we have the case where there was a greater change in the environment, with about 740 cells modified for pasture. However, in another case, the volume of water was higher where the change occurred predominantly in cells with native field uses (increased consumption), and agriculture and forest (reduced consumption).

Scenarios 5, 6, and 7 varied the number and intentions of agents. The number of agents directly interfered with the speed at which changes in land use occurred. The more agents involved in the system, the more changes occurred. In addition, the volume of water had lower final values (in the module) in scenario 5, and higher (in the module) in scenario 7.

In scenario 5, with 2 agents, the biggest change occurred in the case where the intentions were exposed soil (roughly 300 modified cells) and forest (roughly 130 modified cells). In this case, the water volume became negative and decreased. However, another situation generated higher water consumption (see Fig. 6(b)). Overall, out of 10 simulations this scenario presented 4 with negative final water volume and 6 with positive final water volume. In situations where the volume of water was negative, the intentions involved agriculture or exposed soil. However, when the simulation involved these two intentions, but the changes were smaller for these uses, the system demanded less water. In Fig. 6 there are graphs of the volume of water for two cases.

In scenario 6, 5 agents modified the environment. Among the 10 simulations, the final water volume was positive in 6, and negative in 4. However, 2 simulations presented negative values and positive values for the volume of water. Depending on how the environment is modified, the volume of water does not recover, which is devastating for the region. In other cases, the volume of water becomes high, which could also have serious consequences for the environment. To observe this evidence more clearly, we have in Table 3 (simulation 6), which contains the intentions defined in each simulation and the approximate total water volume at the end of the simulation. P represents the pasture land use; A is agriculture land use; E is exposed soil land use; and F is forest land use.

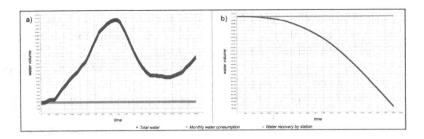

Fig. 6. Graphs of water in the environment, with intentions: (a) forest (roughly 350 modified cells) and agriculture (roughly 50 modified cells); and agriculture (roughly 185 modified cells) and pasture (roughly 105 modified cells).

Table 3. Results in each simulation of scenario 6.

Simulation	Intentions	Water volume
01	P P P A E	250.000
02	P P A E F	−630.000
03	P A F F F	430.000
04	P A F F F	670.000
05	P P A E F	345.000
06	P A E F F	375.000
07	P E E E F	−195.000
08	P P A E E	−520.000
09	P A A F F	−320.000
10	P A E F F	250.000

At each cycle, agents can modify at most one cell contained in one of their own sub-watersheds, but this change does not necessarily take place. In addition, agents are initially positioned in one of their sub-basins, not being considered a fixed position. These two factors interfere in the total change in the environment, which varies according to the possibility, amount and type of modified land use. Thus, the results show that the impact on the environment depends on the intention to change, and also on the total change in each land use. It is shown in Fig. 7, where there are the same intentions for change (pasture (2 agents), agriculture (1 agent), exposed soil (1 agent) and forest (1 agent)). In simulation 02, the biggest changes occur for agriculture and exposed soil. As these two land uses are the ones that consume the most water (Table 1), and the final amount of water in the environment decreases drastically. In simulation 05, the number of water increases, since the greatest change occurs for pasture, which is considered the use with the lowest consumption of water in the system.

In simulations 03 and 05, the environment suffered a drop in the volume of water. However, both environments recovered, according to the need for water consumption from the changes in land use involved. It indicates the possibility of

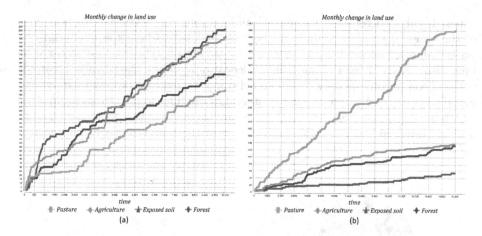

Fig. 7. Change in land use in: (a) simulation 02 and (b) simulation 05.

obtaining a stabilized environment, according to the balance of water consumption between land uses. The simulation that had the greatest change in land use was the third, with about 980 modified cells, followed by the seventh simulation, with about 810 modified cells. Figure 8 shows the final environments of these two simulations. The simulations that generated greater impacts on the volume of water were the second and fourth, with approximately 670 and 770 modified cells, respectively. In this sense, it can be seen that the greatest changes in the environment were not necessarily the ones that generated the greatest consequences in the total volume of water in the environment.

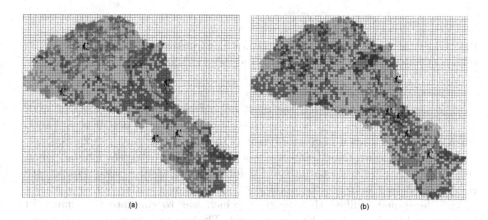

Fig. 8. Final environment in: (a) simulation 03 and (b) simulation 07.

Among the 7 scenarios presented, the case that generated the greatest change in land use was the one that had a modification of approximately 740 cells for exposed soil, 580 cells for the forest, and 80 cells for pasture. This was one of the cases of scenario 7 and can be seen in Fig. 9, where the environment, water volume, and land use change graphs are shown. The smallest water volume also occurred in a simulation of scenario 7, where the change involved exposed soil (approximately 450 modified cells), agriculture (approximately 370 modified cells) and forest (approximately 120 modified cells). In scenario 7, 6 simulations generated negative and decreasing water volume. In addition, 5 simulations involved the 4 possible land uses, 3 of them with negative final water volume.

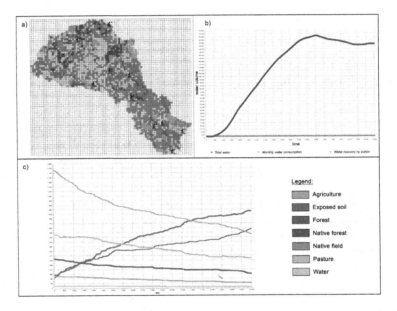

Fig. 9. Results for the simulation with the most land use change: (a) environment; (b) volume of water; and (c) amount of each land use.

The regions that generated the most impact on the volume of water were not necessarily the ones that had the greatest change in land use. In most cases, when cells were modified in greater quantity for agricultural uses or exposed soil, the water volume decreased and was not recovered. On the other hand, when the biggest changes were to pasture or forest, the system tended to decrease consumption and increase the volume of water. The results showed that the MABS developed fulfilled the objective, which was to simulate the change in land use and the impact on the environment. The analyses show that the system had good results from the developed MABS and its rules. In the next section, some conclusions and future works are presented, where some challenges and proposals for improvements in the model are commented on.

4   Conclusion

This work presented a study of land use management in AFW using MABS. The model was developed and simulated on the GAMA platform, from which it was possible to implement data from the study region. Some scenarios were determined from the cases of random intent or not, and from the modification in the number of agents. To verify the results, the graphs, the changes in land use involved, and the respective water costs were analysed with the expected results and each scenario.

Through the simulations of the actions of the agents on the environment, it was possible to visualize the changes in land use at each cycle. In addition, graphs presented the results of the total water volume in the environment and of the final amounts of each land use. Thus, the MABS in GAMA generated an initial study, which in the future may serve as a support tool for the decision makings of land use management. The results from the system and agents rules were satisfactory, and the change in the environment occurred as expected. However, some difficulties were faced from the development and simulation of the model, such as the determination of parameters, the computational time, and the validation.

The model data, such as water volume and water recovery rate, were based on real data. However, the values were adjusted so that the model was better calibrated. Also, seasonal water recovery rates were defined as constant values. In future works, it is expected to develop a tool that more effectively simulates the hydrological behavior of the model. For this, it is intended to couple the MABS to a hydrological model, which will simulate the behavior of the hydrological processes involved in the region.

Another challenge faced was the computational time of the model. The simulation proved to be fast for simulations of up to 10000 cyclings. However, in some cases where the simulations had more cycles, some graphs were not generated. A future objective will be to be able to simulate land use change across the environment, to determine the volume of water at the end of the simulation and the runtime. In addition, it is expected to obtain a model for watersheds with larger areas, in order to explore other important water catchment regions. For this, more data, rules and information in the system will be considered.

In this work, the agents interacted only with the environment. With this, it was possible to explore the division of sub-watersheds by agents, the number of managers, the change in land use in each cell, and the change in the environment according to the variables involved. However, it is important that in future works agents can communicate and cooperate to achieve their goals. This way, agents will be able to act and make decisions about land use management. Also, some characteristics can be determined to managers, such as production rate, cost per product, and the possibility of modifying land use in sub-watersheds of neighboring managers. Thus, the system would have rules that are more solid and closer to reality. In addition, in order to validate the model, it is expected to analyse trends in land use change over the last few years. With this, agents will have intentions that follow trends in specific AFW regions. From this, other studies can be explored.

References

1. Caldeira, T.L., Mello, C.R., Beskow, S., Timm, L.C., Viola, M.R.: LASH hydrological model: an analysis focused on spatial discretization. CATENA **173**, 183–193 (2019). https://doi.org/10.1016/j.catena.2018.10.009
2. Corral, J., et al.: Multi-agent systems applied to land use and social changes in Rio De La Plata Basin (South America). In: 8th European IFSA Symposium, 6–10 July 2008, Clermond-Ferrand (2008). https://ifsa.boku.ac.at/cms/index.php?id=58&L=0
3. Crooks, A.T., Heppenstall, A.J.: Introduction to agent-based modelling. In: Heppenstall, A.J., Crooks, A.T., See, L.M., Batty, M. (eds.) Agent-Based Models of Geographical Systems, pp. 85–105. Springer, Netherlands (2012). https://doi.org/10.1007/978-90-481-8927-4_5
4. Farias, G., Leitzke, B., Born, M., Aguiar, M., Adamatti, D.: Water resources analysis: an approach based on agent-based modeling. Revista de Informática Teórica e Aplicada **27**(2), 81–95 (2020). https://doi.org/10.22456/2175-2745.94319
5. Ganaie, T.A., Jamal, S., Ahmad, W.S.: Changing land use/land cover patterns and growing human population in Wular catchment of Kashmir Valley, India. GeoJournal **86**(4), 1589–1606 (2020). https://doi.org/10.1007/s10708-020-10146-y
6. Gaudou, B., et al.: The MAELIA multi-agent platform for integrated assessment of low-water management issues. In: Alam, S.J., Dyke Parunak, H.V. (eds.) International Workshop on Multi-Agent-Based Simulation (MABS 2013), vol. 8235, pp. 85–110. Springer, Lecture Notes in Computer (2014)
7. Gilbert, N., Troitzsch, K.: Simulation for the Social Scientist. Open University Press, Buckingham (2005)
8. IBGE Homepage: Soil map of sheet SI.22 - Lagoa Mirim. Instituto Brasileiro de Geografia e Estatística (2020). https://dados.gov.br/. Accessed 20 Jan 2020
9. Le Ber, F., Chevrier, V., Dury, A.: A multi-agent system for the simulation of land use organization. IFAC Proc. Vol. **31**(5), 169–174 (1998)
10. Leitzke, B., Adamatti, D.: Multiagent system and rainfall-runoff model in hydrological problems: a systematic literature review. Water **13**(24), 3643 (2021). https://doi.org/10.3390/w13243643
11. Li, M., Cao, X., Liu, D., Fu, Q., Li, T., Shang, R.: Sustainable management of agricultural water and land resources under changing climate and socio-economic conditions: a multi-dimensional optimization approach. Agric. Water Manag. **259**, 107235 (2022). https://doi.org/10.1016/j.agwat.2021.107235
12. Mariano, D.J.K., Alves, C.M.A.: The application of role-playing games and agent-based modelling to the collaborative water management in peri-urban communities. RBRH **25** (2020). https://doi.org/10.1590/2318-0331.252020190100
13. Parker, D.C., Manson, S.M., Janssen, M.A., Hoffmann, M.J., Deadman, P.: Multi-agent systems for the simulation of land-use and land-cover change: a review. Ann. Assoc. Am. Geogr. **93**(2), 314–337 (2003). https://doi.org/10.1111/1467-8306.9302004
14. Russell, S., Norvig, P.: Artificial Intelligence: A Modern Approach. Prentice Hall, New Jersey (2002)

15. She, J., Guan, Z., Cai, F., Pu, L., Tan, J., Chen, T.: Simulation of land use changes in a coastal reclaimed area with dynamic shorelines. Sustainability **9**(3), 431 (2017). https://doi.org/10.3390/su9030431
16. Taillandier, P., et al.: Building, composing and experimenting complex spatial models with the GAMA platform. GeoInformatica **23**(2), 299–322 (2018). https://doi.org/10.1007/s10707-018-00339-6
17. Vicario, S.A., et al.: Unravelling the influence of human behaviour on reducing casualties during flood evacuation. Hydrol. Sci. J. **65**(14), 2359–2375 (2020). https://doi.org/10.1080/02626667.2020.1810254
18. Yamashita, R., Hoshino, S.: Development of an agent-based model for estimation of agricultural land preservation in rural Japan. Agric. Syst. **164**, 264–276 (2018)

Replacing Method for Multi-Agent Crowd Simulation by Convolutional Neural Network

Yu Yamashita[1,2(✉)], Shunki Takami[1,2], Shusuke Shigenaka[1,2], Masaki Onishi[2], and Atsuyuki Morishima[1]

[1] University of Tsukuba, Tsukuba, Japan
yu.yamashita.2021b@mlab.info,
morishima-office@ml.cc.tsukuba.ac.jp
[2] National Institute of Advanced Industrial Science and Technology, Tsukuba, Japan
{s-takami,shusuke-shigenaka,onishi-masaki}@aist.go.jp

Abstract. Multi-agent crowd simulations are used to analyze crowd flows. However, there is a critical problem that the computational time increases with the number of agents because these simulations are based on the interaction of the agents. The approach of using deep neural networks is effective in some applications, such as fluid dynamics simulations. We propose a method of using convolutional neural networks to estimate simulation results from the conditions of each agent and the initial arrangement of a crowd. We evaluated our proposed method through evacuation simulation and demonstrated that our proposed method could obtain evacuation simulation results with high speed.

Keywords: Multi-agent crowd simulation · Convolutional neural network · Evacuation simulation

1 Introduction

Multi-agent crowd simulations are used to analyze crowd flows. These simulations can allow each agent to have conditions, such as a walking speed and route, and compute crowd flows under specific situations. For example, according to previous works, simulations can be used to compute crowd flows during the evacuation from buildings [7, 12, 27, 31]. While the computations in these works are non-interactive, they should be performed with high speed if they are to be used more adaptively.

There is a critical problem that the computational time increases with the number of agents because these simulations are based on the interaction of the agents. Obtaining results with high speed via these simulations is difficult. Nonetheless, no study has addressed this problem, and therefore, a method capable of obtaining simulation results with high speed is required.

The approach of using deep neural networks (DNNs) for simulations has been proposed in some fields, such as fluid dynamics simulations [11, 26] and molecular dynamics simulations [4]. These works have demonstrated that this approach can obtain simulation results with high speed, indicating that it is effective for the problem, and therefore, we use DNNs in this study.

F. Lorig and E. Norling (Eds.): MABS 2022, LNAI 13743, pp. 16–27, 2023.
https://doi.org/10.1007/978-3-031-22947-3_2

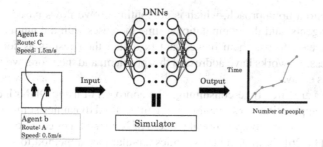

Fig. 1. Our problem setting

This work estimates simulation results from the conditions of each agent and the initial arrangement of a crowd. In this work, we assume the evacuation of a crowd from a building. Given the conditions of each agent (such as the route and the speed) and the initial arrangement of the crowd, we estimate the transition in the number of evacuees over time (Fig. 1). We propose a method that utilizes convolution neural networks (CNNs), which are DNNs. CNNs can extract effective spatial features of crowds and deal with multiple conditions (channels). In addition, we convert from the conditions of each agent and the initial arrangement of a crowd to a structure suited for CNNs. Our goal is to replace the simulation computation process with CNNs to obtain the results with high speed.

We evaluated the effectiveness of our proposed method in terms of estimation accuracy and speed. For this purpose, we used simulation data on evacuation settings in a theater. We show that our proposed method performs evacuation simulations 50 times faster than the simulator, with high accuracy simulation results. Our experimental results show that our proposed method can obtain simulation results with high speed.

Our contributions are summarized as follows:

1. We first address the critical problem of increasing computational time with the number of agents in multi-agent crowd simulations.
2. We propose a method that uses CNNs, which are DNNs, to tackle the above problem. CNNs can extract effective spatial features of crowds and deal with multiple conditions (channels).
3. We evaluated our proposed method through evacuation simulation and demonstrated that our proposed method could obtain evacuation simulation results with high speed.

2 Related Work

Several works have been conducted to compute traffic flows [2,15,20,24], and human behaviors [16] through multi-agent simulations. In this work, we deal with multi-agent simulations to compute crowd flows (multi-agent crowd simulations) [29]. For example, these simulations have computed the evacuation of crowd in buildings [7,31], aircrafts [19], airports [27], and cities [12]. Simulation systems cosidering geographical information [28] and human behavioral parameters [18] are proposed. These simulations employ the bottom-up approach, which is computing crowd flows based on the inter-action on the agents, and the computational time increases with the number of agents. Thus, it is not easy to use them if we want to obtain their results as soon as possible. Nonetheless, no works have addressed this problem, and therefore, we address this problem in this study.

Simulations are often time-consuming. The approach of using DNNs has been proposed in some applications to solve this problem. In fluid dynamics simulations, methods to replace part of the computational process of Navier-Stokes equations with CNNs are proposed [11,26]. In molecular dynamics simulations, a method to estimate long-term simulation results from using short-term simulation results by using DNNs is proposed. These works have shown that this approach can obtain simulation results with high speed, which indicates it is effective for the problem. These simulations and the multi-agent crowd simulation are the same in that they compute complex phenomena composed of numerous elements, and therefore, we use DNNs in this study.

CNNs have made great progress mainly in the image domain (image recognition [23], image segmentation [1], object detection [17], and pose estimation [3]). These networks have convolutional and pooling layers, extract effective spatial features, and deal with multiple channels. They have recently been applied not only in the image domain but also in other fields, such as natural language processing [6], acoustic signal processing [14], and game AI [22]. Several works succeeded in predicting future crowd flows with high accuracy by extracting spatial features of the current crowds using CNNs [10,13,25,30]. The initial arrangement of a crowd significantly impacts future crowd flows in multi-agent crowd simulations, and therefore, we use CNNs.

3   Problem Setting

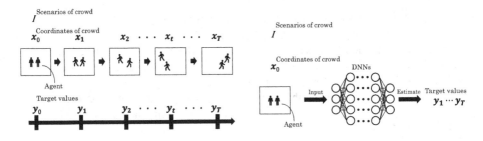

Fig. 2. General setting in multi-agent crowd simulation

Fig. 3. Our setting

Figure 2 shows the general setting in multi-agent crowd simulation. The scenarios of the crowd I define the behavior of the crowd and are composed of multiple conditions such as route and speed [5,9]. The coordinates of the crowd $x_{t \in T}$ indicates the position of the crowd at the timestamp $t \in T$ and has horizontal and vertical values, respectively. Given the scenarios of the crowd I and the initial coordinates of the crowd x_0, the simulator computes the coordinates of the crowd $x_1, \cdots, x_T$ and outputs the target values $y_1, \cdots, y_T$. The rectangle in Fig. 2 shows the snapshot of the crowd created in the simulator based on the coordinates of the crowd x_t.

4 Proposed Method

In this work, we estimate target values $y_1, \cdots, y_T$ from the scenarios of the crowd I and the initial coordinates of the crowd x_0 (Fig. 3). We propose a method of using CNNs to extract effective spatial features of crowds since the initial arrangement of a crowd has a significant impact on future crowd flows in multi-agent crowd simulations. In addition, we convert the conditions of each agent and the initial arrangement of a crowd to a three-dimensional tensor (3d-tensor) suited for CNNs. Our method consists of two steps: (1) converting the set of scenarios I and the initial coordinates x_0 to a 3d-tensor and (2) estimating target values $y_1, \cdots, y_T$ by using CNNs.

We use a multi-agent crowd simulator to generate several sets of pairs of scenarios I, a set of initial coordinates x_0, and target values $y_1, \cdots, y_T$. These are used as a dataset for training CNNs.

4.1 Conversion to 3d-Tensor

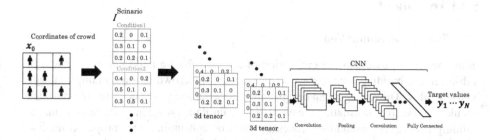

Fig. 4. Conversion to a 3d-tensor

Fig. 5. Estimation by using convolutional neural networks (CNNs)

We convert the scenarios of the crowd I and the initial coordinates of the crowd x_0 to a 3d-tensor (Fig. 4). First, we develop a two-dimensional tensor (2d-tensor) for each condition and each value, which is assigned an arbitrary value according to the conditions of the agent existing at that coordinate. Then, we develop 2d-tensors for the number of conditions and stack them in the channel direction to develop a 3d-tensor $z \in \mathbb{R}^{d_1 \times d_2 \times d_3}$. For example, if the scenario consists of speed, route, and departure time, we develop a 3d-tensor with three channels. A 3d-tensor is a structure suited for CNNs and can retain features of the initial coordinates and the scenario composed of multiple conditions. These features are essential for estimating target values because simulations are based on them.

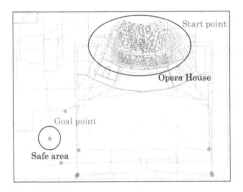

Fig. 6. Starting point and goal point of evacuation

4.2 Estimation by Using CNNs

CNNs output target values $y_1, \cdots, y_T$ from the scenarios of the crowd I and the initial coordinates of the crowd x_0 (Fig. 5). CNNs are composed of convolutional and pooling layers and are applied in several domains. CNNs have two advantages: (1) extracting effective spatial features of crowds and (2) dealing with multiple conditions (channels).

5   Experiment

5.1   Evacuation Simulation

In this work, we assumed the evacuation of a crowd from a building. In the event of a disaster, the building manager wants to evacuate the crowd in the building to a safe area smoothly. The manager can design various evacuation guidance guidelines through simulations (such as estimating the elapsed time until the crowd has evacuated from the building); however, simulation processes are time-consuming. Our proposed method enables the manager to plan the best guidance for daily situations by reducing the computation time of simulations.

We assumed The New National Theatre, Tokyo, as the building in this study. We used CrowdWalk as a multi-agent crowd simulator. The evacuation of the crowd was computed based on an actual evacuation drill in the theater by using CrowdWalk [25]. The crowd is in the Opera House, which is defined as the start point, and evacuates to a safe area, which is defined as the goal point (Fig. 6).

The scenario is composed of four conditions: s_1 the time to start the evacuation, s_2 the exit door of the Opera House, s_3 the route for the evacuation, and s_4 the walking speed. s_1 to s_3 are based on the guidance by the staff of the theater. s_4 are dependent on the people characters, such as the elderly, children, the public, and wheelchair users. The condition s_1 indicates the time to start evacuation in seconds from a point in time after a disaster occurs. The target values $y_1, \cdots, y_T$ indicate the elapsed times for the number of people who have arrived at the goal point to reach $10t\%$ of the total number of people. Let $T = 10$ and $0 \leq t \leq 10$. We indicate the transition in the

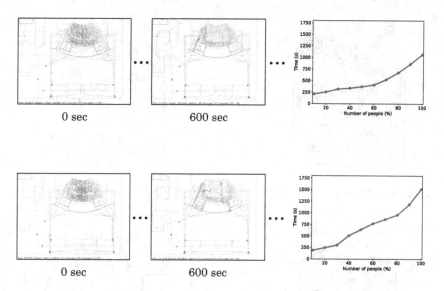

Fig. 7. Snapshots of an evacuation simulation and transitions in the number of evacuees over time

number of evacuees over time by connecting the elapsed times $y_1, \cdots, y_T$. Figure 7 shows snapshots of the crowd created in the simulator based on the coordinates of the crowd and transitions in the number of evacuees. Given the scenarios of the crowd I composed of four conditions and the initial coordinates of the crowd x_0, the simulator computes the coordinates of the crowd $x_1, \cdots, x_T$ based on the scenarios of the crowd I and outputs the elapsed times (the transition in the number of evacuees over time) $y_1, \cdots, y_T$. Therefore, we estimated the elapsed times $y_1, \cdots, y_T$ from the scenarios of the crowd I and the initial coordinates of the crowd x_0 in this experiment.

5.2 Dataset Setting

We gave the various scenarios of the crowd and initial coordinates of the crowd and let the simulator output the elapsed times for this experiment. We obtained 60,000 sets of scenarios of the crowd, the initial coordinates of the crowd, and the elapsed times.

The Opera House has 22 horizontal columns and up to 42 vertical columns. Figure 8 and Fig. 9 show the Opera House, divided by seats and blocks.

Initial Coordinates of the Crowd I: For 30% of samples of all data, agents were generated randomly for each seat ranging from 0 to no greater than the maximum number of people allowed to sit in that seat (Fig. 8). For 70% of samples of all data, $\alpha \in \{0.4, 0.7, 1.0\}$ was chosen randomly for each block, and agents were generated randomly for seats in that block with the maximum number of people$\times \alpha$ (Fig. 9).

Time to Start Evacuation s_1: The time to start is within $\{0, 30, \cdots, 300\}$. For 10% of samples of all data, the time was set 0 s for all agents. For 20% of samples of all data, the time was chosen randomly for each seat (Fig. 8). For 70% of samples of all data, the

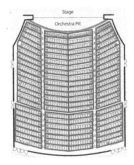

Fig. 8. Opera House divided by seats

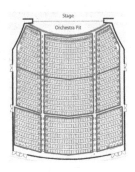

Fig. 9. Opera House divided by blocks

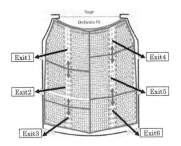

Fig. 10. Exit from Opera House

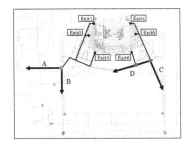

Fig. 11. Evacuation routes guidance

time was chosen randomly for each block (Fig. 9). It was assumed that at least one seat agents start evacuation at 0 s.

Door to Exit the Opera House Through s_2: Six exiting doors are within Exit 1–6 (Fig. 10). Agents on the left half of the Opera House exited through one of Exit 1–3, and agents on the right half exited through one of Exit 4–6. Two boundaries were set randomly on the left half and right half, and agents sitting in front of the first boundary exited from Exit 1 (left half) or Exit 4 (right half), agents sitting between the first and second boundaries exited from Exit 2 (left half) or Exit 5 (right half), and agents sitting behind the second boundary exited from Exit 3 (left half) or Exit 6 (right half).

Route to Evacuate Through s_3: Agents exiting from the Opera House through Exit 1–3 evacuated through route A or B, and agents exiting through Exit 4–6 evacuated through route C or D (Fig. 11). The rates of routes A and B, along with C and D, were randomly set, and the route was chosen based on each rate.

Walking Speed s_4: There are three-speed types: the default speed of CrowdWalk, 1.5 and 0.5 times faster than the default speed. We assumed that the first speed is the average speed of typical adults, the second speed is the average speed of young people, and the third speed is the average speed of older people or wheelchair users. For 30% of samples of all data, the speed was randomly chosen for each seat (Fig. 8). For 70% of samples of all data, the speed was randomly chosen for each block (Fig. 9).

5.3   Conversion to 3d-Tensor

We converted the scenarios of the crowd I composed of four conditions and the initial coordinates of the crowd x_0 to a 3d-tensor. First, we developed a 2d-tensor for each condition and value, which was assigned an arbitrary value according to the condition of the agent that existed at that coordinate. In a tensor of the time to start evacuation s_1, agents starting evacuation at 0, 30, ... , 300 s later were assigned 1, 2, ... , 11, respectively. In a tensor of the door to exit the Opera House through s_2, agents exiting through the doors Exit 1, Exit 2, ... , Exit 6 were assigned 1, 2, ... , 6, respectively. In a tensor of the route to evacuate through s_3, agents evacuating through routes A, B, C, and D were assigned 1, 2, 3, and 4, respectively. In a tensor of the walking speed s_4, agents walking at 0.5 times faster than the default speed, the default speed, and 1.5 times faster than the default speed were assigned 1, 2, and 3, respectively. The values of tensors with no agents were assigned 0, and we multiplied all values by 0.1 following the standard techniques of DNNs [21]. Then, we stacked these developed 2d-tensors in the channel direction to develop a 3d-tensor $z \in \mathbb{R}^{d_1 \times d_2 \times d_3}$, thus we obtained a 3d-tensor of $4 \times 22 \times 42$.

5.4   Estimation Using CNNs

CNNs output the elapsed times (the transition in the number of evacuees over time) from the 3d-tensor. We used ResNet-50 [8], which is a typical CNN. ResNet has a residual module that includes a shortcut to pass $H(a) = F(a) + a$ to the next layer. The residual module has a shortcut that allows the gradient to be passed directly to lower layers during backpropagation. This prevents the gradient from vanishing even in a network with very deep layers and enables efficient learning.

We used root mean squared error (RMSE) as the error function of the output layer of the CNN and Adam as the optimization function with $\beta_1 = 0.9$, $\beta_2 = 0.999$, and $\epsilon = 10^{-8}$. The number of the epoch was set to 200, and the learning rate was first set to 0.001 and multiplied by 0.5 for 60, 120, and 160 epochs. The batch size was set to 256.

We split all data into training data (40,000), validation data (10,000), and test data (10,000).

6   Result

We evaluated the estimation accuracy, the multiple conditions dealing ability, and the estimation speed. We show that our proposed method can estimate simulation results with high speed and accuracy and deal with multiple conditions based on experimental results.

First, we evaluated the estimation accuracy. The error (RMSE) for the test data was 34.157. Figure 12 shows six randomly selected estimated and true elapsed times (the transitions in the number of evacuees over time) for the test data. The blue and orange colors indicate the estimated true transitions, respectively. The horizontal axis shows the percentage of people who have arrived at the goal point, and the vertical axis shows the elapsed times for each figure. These results show that the estimated and

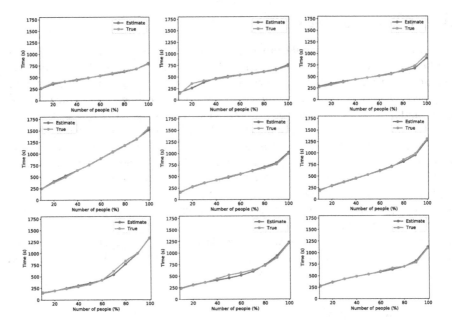

Fig. 12. Estimated and true elapsed times. The blue color indicates the estimated transition and the orange color indicates the true transition. The horizontal axis shows the percentage of people who have arrived at the goal point, and the vertical axis shows the elapsed times for each figure. (Color figure online)

Table 1. Average loss for number of condition types

Number of condition types	Average loss (RMSE)
1	116.607
2	98.879
3	75.207
4	**34.157**

true elapsed times almost overlap, indicating that the proposed method can estimate simulation results with high accuracy.

Second, we evaluated the multiple conditions dealing ability. The ability indicates whether our proposed method could train from multiple conditions. We compared the average loss (RMSE) when the number of condition types was varied from 1 to 4 (Table 1). The number of channels was set to be four even if the number of condition types was different (Fig. 13). For example, when the number of condition types is one, a 3d-tensor is composed of four s_1, s_2, or others. When the number of condition types is two, a 3d-tensor is composed of two s_1 and two s_2, two s_3 and two s_4, or others. We developed all possible combinations of conditions and averaged the loss (RMSE) for the number of condition types. The result shows that the average loss decreases as

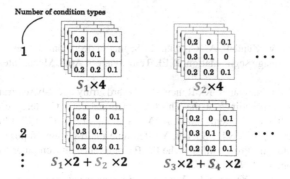

Fig. 13. 3d-tensors for number of condition types

Table 2. Time taken to output a result using the proposed method and the simulation

Simulator (CrowdWalk)	Our proposed method
8.223 (s)	**0.161 (s)**

the number of conditions increases, and it is minimum for all conditions (the number of condition types is 4) These indicate that the proposed method can deal with scenarios composed of multiple conditions.

Finally, we evaluated the estimation speed. We compared the time taken to output a result using the proposed method and simulation (Table 2). The simulation was computed on an Intel i7-5930K CPU. From measurement results, it took approximately 8.223 s on average. Our proposed method was computed on a TITAN RTX with 24 GB. From measurement results, it took approximately 0.161 s on average. Therefore, the proposed method could estimate approximately 50 times faster than the simulation. This indicates that the proposed method could obtain the results with high speed. The estimation time of the proposed method is independent of the simulation time.

In this study, we use DNNs to estimate simulation results with high speed. DNNs perform with high accuracy in using large training data, target samples interpolated into the training data. Therefore, it is desirable to have large and comprehensive training data. A situation in which the training data are limited is a future challenge.

Based on the results, we conclude that our proposed method replaces the simulation computation process and enables us to rapidly obtain simulation results.

7 Conclusion

We addressed the critical problem that the time to compute increases with the number of agents in multi-agent crowd simulations. We proposed a method using CNNs to estimate simulation results from the conditions of each agent and the initial arrangement of the crowd. We evaluated our proposed method via evacuation simulations and demonstrated that our proposed method enables us to obtain evacuation simulation results with high speed.

References

1. Badrinarayanan, V., Kendall, A., Cipolla, R.: Segnet: a deep convolutional encoder-decoder architecture for image segmentation. IEEE Trans. Pattern Anal. Mach. Intell. **39**(12), 2481–2495 (2017)
2. Balmer, M., Cetin, N., Nagel, K., Raney, B.: Towards truly agent-based traffic and mobility simulations. In: Proceedings of the Third International Joint Conference on Autonomous Agents and Multiagent Systems, 2004. AAMAS 2004, pp. 60–67. IEEE (2004)
3. Cao, Z., Simon, T., Wei, S.E., Sheikh, Y.: Realtime multi-person 2d pose estimation using part affinity fields. In: Proceedings of the IEEE Conference on Computer Vision and Pattern Recognition, pp. 7291–7299 (2017)
4. Endo, K., Tomobe, K., Yasuoka, K.: Multi-step time series generator for molecular dynamics. In: Thirty-Second AAAI Conference on Artificial Intelligence (2018)
5. Feng, Y., Duives, D., Daamen, W., Hoogendoorn, S.: Data collection methods for studying pedestrian behaviour: a systematic review. Build. Environ. **187**, 107329 (2021)
6. Gehring, J., Auli, M., Grangier, D., Yarats, D., Dauphin, Y.N.: Convolutional sequence to sequence learning. In: International Conference on Machine Learning, pp. 1243–1252. PMLR (2017)
7. Gianni, D., Loukas, G., Gelenbe, E., et al.: A simulation framework for the investigation of adaptive behaviours in largely populated building evacuation scenarios. In: Proceedings of the Seventh International Joint Conference on Autonomous Agents and Multi-Agent Systems (AAMAS 08), Estoril, Portugal, vol. 1216. Citeseer (2008)
8. He, K., Zhang, X., Ren, S., Sun, J.: Deep residual learning for image recognition. In: Proceedings of the IEEE Conference on Computer Vision and Pattern Recognition, pp. 770–778 (2016)
9. Hoogendoorn, S.P., Bovy, P.H.: Pedestrian route-choice and activity scheduling theory and models. Transp. Res. Part B: Methodol. **38**(2), 169–190 (2004)
10. Jiang, R., et al.: Deepurbanevent: a system for predicting citywide crowd dynamics at big events. In: Proceedings of the 25th ACM SIGKDD International Conference on Knowledge Discovery & Data Mining, pp. 2114–2122 (2019)
11. Kochkov, D., Smith, J.A., Alieva, A., Wang, Q., Brenner, M.P., Hoyer, S.: Machine learning-accelerated computational fluid dynamics. Proc. Natl. Acad. Sci. **118**(21), e2101784118 (2021)
12. Lämmel, G., Rieser, M., Nagel, K.: Bottlenecks and congestion in evacuation scenarios: A microscopic evacuation simulation for large-scale disasters. In: Proc. of 7th Int. Conf. on Autonomous Agents and Multiagent Systems (AAMAS 2008), Estoril, Portugal (2008)
13. Liang, Y., et al.: Urbanfm: inferring fine-grained urban flows. In: Proceedings of the 25th ACM SIGKDD International Conference on Knowledge Discovery & Data Mining, pp. 3132–3142 (2019)
14. Oord, A., et al.: Parallel wavenet: fast high-fidelity speech synthesis. In: International Conference on Machine Learning, pp. 3918–3926. PMLR (2018)
15. Paruchuri, P., Pullalarevu, A.R., Karlapalem, K.: Multi agent simulation of unorganized traffic. In: Proceedings of the First International Joint Conference on Autonomous Agents and Multiagent Systems: part 1, pp. 176–183 (2002)
16. Rasouli, A.: Pedestrian simulation: A review. arXiv preprint arXiv:2102.03289 (2021)
17. Redmon, J., Farhadi, A.: Yolo9000: better, faster, stronger. In: Proceedings of the IEEE Conference on Computer Vision and Pattern Recognition, pp. 7263–7271 (2017)
18. Sharma, S.: Avatarsim: a multi-agent system for emergency evacuation simulation. J. Comput. Meth. Sci. Eng. **9**(s1), S13–S22 (2009)

19. Sharma, S., Singh, H., Prakash, A.: Multi-agent modeling and simulation of human behavior in aircraft evacuations. IEEE Trans. Aerosp. Electron. Syst. **44**(4), 1477–1488 (2008)
20. Sharon, G., et al.: Real-time adaptive tolling scheme for optimized social welfare in traffic networks. In: Proceedings of the 16th International Conference on Autonomous Agents and Multiagent Systems (AAMAS-2017) (2017)
21. Shorten, C., Khoshgoftaar, T.M.: A survey on image data augmentation for deep learning. J. Big Data **6**(1), 1–48 (2019)
22. Silver, D., et al.: Mastering the game of go without human knowledge. Nature **550**(7676), 354–359 (2017)
23. Simonyan, K., Zisserman, A.: Very deep convolutional networks for large-scale image recognition. arXiv preprint arXiv:1409.1556 (2014)
24. Singh, A.J., Nguyen, D.T., Kumar, A., Lau, H.C.: Multiagent decision making for maritime traffic management. In: Proceedings of the AAAI Conference on Artificial Intelligence, vol. 33, pp. 6171–6178 (2019)
25. Takeuchi, K., Nishida, R., Kashima, H., Onishi, M.: Grab the reins of crowds: Estimating the effects of crowd movement guidance using causal inference. arXiv preprint arXiv:2102.03980 (2021)
26. Tompson, J., Schlachter, K., Sprechmann, P., Perlin, K.: Accelerating eulerian fluid simulation with convolutional networks. In: International Conference on Machine Learning, pp. 3424–3433. PMLR (2017)
27. Tsai, J., et al.: ESCAPES: evacuation simulation with children, authorities, parents, emotions, and social comparison. In: AAMAS, vol. 11, pp. 457–464 (2011)
28. Uno, K., Kashiyama, K.: Development of simulation system for the disaster evacuation based on multi-agent model using GIS. Tsinghua Sci. Technol. **13**(S1), 348–353 (2008)
29. Yamashita, T., Okada, T., Noda, I.: Implementation of simulation environment for exhaustive analysis of huge-scale pedestrian flow. SICE J. Control Meas. Syst. Integr. **6**(2), 137–146 (2013)
30. Zhang, J., Zheng, Y., Qi, D.: Deep spatio-temporal residual networks for citywide crowd flows prediction. In: Thirty-first AAAI Conference on Artificial Intelligence (2017)
31. Zhou, M., Dong, H., Ioannou, P.A., Zhao, Y., Wang, F.Y.: Guided crowd evacuation: approaches and challenges. IEEE/CAA J. Automatica Sinica **6**(5), 1081–1094 (2019)

An Agent-Based Model of Horizontal Mergers

Martin Harry Vargas Barrenechea[ID] and
José Bruno do Nascimento Clementino[(✉)][ID]

Federal University of Ouro Preto, Mariana, MG, Brazil
`jose.clementino@aluno.ufop.edu.br`

Abstract. This paper is about the agentization of a horizontal mergers model. In this model, firms are either in a differentiated products
Bertrand competition, in which they choose prices in order to maximize
their profits, or in a Cournot competition, in which quantities are chosen by firms. The analytical game theoretical model predicts that once
a firm merges to another, prices of the merging party rise, which leads
to a decrease in consumer surplus and an increase in producer surplus.
Developed along this draft is an agent-based version of this model in
which firms do not know the demand they are facing. We find conver-
gence of our agent-based model to the game theoretical results before and
after firms merge. Alternative learning methods will be implemented as
a further extension to this agent-based model.

Keywords: Horizontal mergers · Agent-based models · Game theory

1 Introduction

A horizontal merger occurs when competitors in an industry merge. Since this
event leads to the concentration of an industry, one of its possible consequences
is the exercise of unilateral market power – which could translate into a raise in
prices not only of the goods involved in merging parties, but of the whole market. According to the Federal Trade Commission, the regulation agency responsible for evaluating mergers in the United States, over a thousand merger cases
are reviewed every year[1]. In Europe, the European Commission (EC) received
around 230 notifications until july of this year[2]. As stated by the Federal Trade
Commission, around 5% of the cases reviewed by the agency present competitive issues. In that case, to prevent mergers that are damaging to the consumer's
welfare and competition, it is necessary to study and develop methods that help
verifying if mergers will affect competition negatively.

A significant amount of methodologies that measure the effects of mergers
have been developed such as [1–3,5]. All of these methods use analytical and

---

[1] See: https://www.ftc.gov/tips-advice/competition-guidance/guide-antitrust-laws/
mergers.

[2] See:https://ec.europa.eu/competition-policy/mergers/statistics_en.

F. Lorig and E. Norling (Eds.): MABS 2022, LNAI 13743, pp. 28–40, 2023.
https://doi.org/10.1007/978-3-031-22947-3_3

statistical tools for the estimation of prices before and after mergers. However, there's an absence of models that describe and reproduce such effects of unilateral market power in the agent-based computational economics literature. Although industrial organization studies the strategic interaction between firms, which could be represented through agent-based modeling tools, [11] states a lack of integration between the industrial organization theory and agent-based methodologies. This paper is a small contribution to narrow the gap between these two research areas.

Using a constructive approach, as proposed by [14], an agent-based model of horizontal mergers is developed. A model presented in [10], where firms are in a differentiated products Bertrand game, is used as a benchmark case and goes through the process of *agentization*, which is also described in [6]. The model is also extended to the Cournot game. Assumptions of perfect rationality and information are relaxed from the model, and the emerging patterns before and after mergers are studied. Under our chosen assumptions of agent learning, qualitative and quantitative results are identical to the analytical model.

The work is divided into four sections. In the first section, the exposition and assumptions of the analytical model are presented. The second section presents the agent-based version of this model. Presented in the third section are the results obtained from simulations. Finally, the fourth has concluding remarks about this work and extensions that we plan to include on a future version.

2   The Analytical Model

As mentioned earlier, this model is largely based on the model of horizontal mergers featured in [10, p.244-265]. To the reader that might not be familiar with the concept of a horizontal merger, these mergers happen whenever firms of the same industry merge[3]. A quick exposition of the model is going to be done in this section, showing the utility of a representative consumer and how it determines quantities given the prices of the goods in the market and how firms, considering this demand, determine optimal prices.

2.1   Bertrand Competition with Differentiated Products

The utility of the representative consumer depends on multiple differentiated products in the market. It is represented as:

$$U = v \sum_{i=1}^{n} q_i - \frac{n}{2+\gamma} \left[\sum_{i=1}^{n} q_i^2 + \frac{\gamma}{n} \left(\sum_{i=1}^{n} q_i \right)^2 \right] + y \tag{1}$$

where y is an outside good, and since this demand is quasi-linear, it does not affect the decisions taken by the consumer with respect to the differentiated products; q_i is the quantity of the i-th product; v is a positive parameter; n is the

---

[3] One alternative would be the occasion in which a firm sells input to another firm that produces a final good. In the case that one firm merges with the other, this event would be called a vertical merger.

number of products in the industry; and γ represents the degree of substitutability between the n products. From utility maximization, prices and quantities can be determined. The direct demand function is defined as:

$$q_i = \frac{1}{n}\left[v - p_i(1 + \gamma) + \frac{\gamma}{n}\sum_{j=1}^{n} p_j\right] \tag{2}$$

Quick inspection shows that the demand for the i-th good depends on its own price and the price of other goods, that is, if a good has a price that is too high, it will be substituted by other products, depending on the degree of substitutability, which will lead to a diminished demand for this product. However, if other goods are too expensive, then the good in question will be purchased abundantly. Another property of this demand function is the fact that the aggregate demand does not depend on the degree of substitution among the products. Finally, if prices are identical among all firms, the aggregate quantity does not change with the number of products that exist in an industry.

This model presumes that each firm in an industry sells a single good. The profit attained from selling each good is defined as:

$$\pi_i = (p_i - c)(q_i) \tag{3}$$

where c is the marginal cost for producing a unit of the i-th good. For simplicity, this model presumes that there are no fixed costs in the cost function and costs are homogeneous among firms. The firm's expected behavior is to choose a price that maximizes its profit. By substituting Eq. 2 on Eq. 3, taking the derivative with respect to price and setting it to zero, the game theoretical price for the i-th good will be:

$$p_i = \frac{nv + \gamma\sum_{j=1, j\neq i}^{n} p_j + c(n + n\gamma - \gamma)}{2(n + n\gamma - \gamma)} \tag{4}$$

When a firm merges to other firms, the merged party turns into a multi-product firm. This new firm sells m products while the remaining firms sell $m-n$ products. The profit of the multi-product firm will be the sum of the attained profits when considering all goods involved in the merge. Game theoretical prices are obtained by taking the derivative of both products and setting it to zero, the results will be:

$$p_I(m) = \frac{c(n\gamma(4n - 2m - 1) + 2n^2 + \gamma^2(2n^2 - nm - 2n - m^2 + 2m)) + nv(2n + \gamma(2n - 1))}{\gamma^2(2n^2 - nm - 2n - m^2 + 2m) + 2\gamma n(3n - m - 1) + 4n^2} \tag{5}$$

$$p_o(m) = \frac{c(n\gamma(4n - m - 2) + 2n^2 + \gamma^2(2n^2 - nm - 2n - m^2 + 2m)) + nv(2n + \gamma(2n - m))}{\gamma^2(2n^2 - nm - 2n - m^2 + 2m) + 2\gamma n(3n - m - 1) + 4n^2} \tag{6}$$

where Eq. 5 is the price of the multi-product firm and Eq. 6 is the price of the outside firm (that is, the firm that is not in the merging party). Notice how both profits are in terms of the products sold by the merging party. The higher the number of products sold by the multi-product firm, the higher are profits for both types of firms. This suggests that the consumer surplus decreases in the presence of a merger[4].

2.2 Cournot Competition with Differentiated Products

In this paper, we also consider the agentization of the Cournot competition with differentiated products model. The utility of the representative agent is identical to the Bertrand case with the exception that instead of inserting Eq. 2 into the profit function, the indirect demand is inserted. This indirect demand is given by the following equation:

$$p_i = v - \frac{1}{1+\gamma}(nq_i + \gamma \sum_{j=1}^{n} q_j) \tag{7}$$

In this model, the firm's expected behavior is to choose a quantity that maximizes its profit. The game theoretical quantity for the i-th good will be given by the following equation:

$$q_i = \frac{(v-c)(1+\gamma) - \gamma \sum_{j=1, j\neq i}^{n} q_j}{2(n+\gamma)} \tag{8}$$

Like the Bertrand case, we consider that a firm merges to other firms, which leads to the creation of a multi-product firm that sells m products. The remaining firms sell $(n - m)$ products. The game theoretical quantities that are obtained from this new market arrangement are given by the following equations:

$$q_I(m) = \frac{(v-c)(1+\gamma)(2n+\gamma)}{(2n+2m\gamma)(2n+\gamma(n-m+1)) - mn\gamma^2 + \gamma^2 m^2} \tag{9}$$

$$q_o(m) = \frac{(v-c)(1+\gamma)[(2n+2m\gamma)(2n+\gamma(n-m+1)) - mn\gamma^2 + \gamma^2 m^2 - 2\gamma(2n+\gamma)]}{(2n+\gamma(n-m+1))((2n+2m\gamma)(2n+\gamma(n-m+1)) - mn\gamma^2 + \gamma^2 m^2)} \tag{10}$$

where Eq. 9 is the quantity sold of each product in the multi-product firm portfolio and Eq. 10 is the quantity sold by firms that are outside of the merging party. These quantities are conceptually similar to the Bertrand case, because it assumes that the firms are in an symmetric equilibrium. However, mergers under a Cournot competition are not necessarily profitable. This happens because merged firms produce a smaller quantity than non-merged firms, and unless products are extremely differentiated, which is associated to a small γ, the firms that are outside the merger will compensate the smaller production from the multi-product firm in order to increase their own profits.

---

[4] To the reader that is unfamiliar with the consumer surplus, it is described as the amount of utility obtained by a consumer after a transaction. A simple formula for it would be $CS = \sum_{i=1}^{n} U(q_i) - q \cdot p$, where q and p are vectors for quantities and prices respectively. With quantities held constant, an increase in prices leads to a decrease in CS.

3   The Agent-Based Model

The last section gave a quick overview regarding the analytical model of mergers. Describing the agentization of the model is the purpose of this section. As is going to be shown through the Overview, Design Concepts, and Details (ODD) protocol based on [13], the agentization of this model is going to occur with respect to firm behavior. Instead of firms that have access to perfect information and rationality, firms are rationally bounded. With this we are effectively relaxing some of the hypotheses of the original model.

Purpose and Patterns

The purpose of the model is to reproduce the game theoretical results of a differentiated products Bertrand competition. Mergers lead to market concentration, which leads to a general increase in prices.

Entities, State Variables and Scales

The entities of the model are firms that are engaged in the competition. In this version of the model, geographic space is not relevant. Simulations are run from 1500 to 4000 periods. Every firm has the following state variables:

- *current price*: from which it draws price bids every period in the Bertrand case;
- *current quantity*: from which it draws quantity bids every period in the Cournot case;
- *cost*: the cost of producing a single good.

Process Overview and Scheduling

In the Bertrand case, at every period, firms draw price bids which determine quantities. After these quantities are determined, profits are calculated and saved on their memories. When prices are stable, firms engage in the merging process and a new price adjustment phase begins. The Cournot case is quite similar to the Bertrand one, the difference is regarding to the bids that are drawn by firms: instead of drawing price bids, firms draw quantity bids. For the sake of simplicity, we focus on the explanation of the Bertrand case.

Design Concepts

Firms try to learn prices that maximize their profits adaptively. Since firms are not able to see information from their competitors, the interaction is only through indirect means because their prices affect demand. From the learning process and adaptation, game theoretical prices emerge.

Initialization

In this version, firms are identical when considering current prices, costs and learning parameters. The only form of heterogeneity in this model is driven by stochasticity, because bids are chosen randomly, and it's not unlikely that bids are distinct from each other. Chosen values for parameters are presented in the following section.

Submodels

Besides the equation that is responsible for determining the demand, another submodel is defined for firm behavior. The learning method is based on [8]. It is an adaptation to a line search method which is useful for finding the optima of functions that have a single variable[5]. Firms draw bids from a uniform distribution:

$$bid \sim U(\text{current price} - \delta, \text{current price} + \delta) \qquad (11)$$

after their bids are drawn, quantities are determined by Eq. 2. The results from their profits are saved into one of two lists: the first one is for when a firm bids higher than its current price; the other list is for when a firm bids lower than its current price. After an "epoch", the name given for a learning phase consisting of 30 periods, the firm compares the mean from both lists. If the list related to high prices has a mean profit higher than the list of low prices, then:

$$new\ current\ price = current\ price + \epsilon \qquad (12)$$

else:

$$new\ current\ price = current\ price - \epsilon \qquad (13)$$

after the firm is done, the lists are emptied and a new learning phase begins. A simple pseudocode, adapted from [8, p.189] is presented for the sake of clarity on algorithm 1.

Another simple submodel for price stability (or equilibrium) is necessary for the initialization of a merger. Stability is defined in terms of moving averages. A moving average considers the current price of three epochs. Let μ_1 be the average of three epochs; after that, μ_2 is defined as the average of the next three epochs. If the absolute value of the difference between these two averages is lower than a threshold, that is $|\mu_2 - \mu_1| \leq \theta$, then prices are stable, which means firms have found an equilibrium. If that is not the case, $\mu_1 = \mu_2$ and a new value of μ_2 is calculated considering the next three epochs.

Because we are interested in the means of current prices before and after mergers, mergers occur only after prices are stable. When two firms merge, the profit of each product is calculated individually, but the firms that are part of the merging party see their profit as the sum of their individual profits.

3.1   Model Implementation and Parameters

The model was implemented using Netlogo v6.2 ([15]). Its parameters used in simulations were the ones given in Table 1.

Under such parameters, the game theoretical (optimal price) is: 11.54, and the optimal quantity associated with that price is: 29.49. After a merger happens, the optimal price for the merging party is: 16.87; for the non-merging firms, the price will be 13.86. For the Cournot case, the Nash equilibrium quantity is 21.43, while price will be 35.71. After a merger happens, the quantity of the

---

[5] See [12] for an overview of the method.

Algorithm 1. Probe and Adjust

1: Set learning parameters: $\delta, \epsilon, epoch\_length$
2: $counter \leftarrow 0$
3: $returns\_up \leftarrow []$ (An empty list associated with current price raises)
4: $returns\_down \leftarrow []$ (An empty list associated with current price decreases)
5: Do forever:
6: $counter \leftarrow counter + 1$
7: $price\_bid \sim U(current\_price - \delta, current\_price + \delta)$
8: $profit \leftarrow$ Return of price_bid
9: **if** $bid\_price \geq current\_price$ **then**
10:     Append profit to returns_up
11: **else**
12:     Append profit to returns_down
13: **end if**
14: **if** $(counter \mod epoch\_length = 0)$ **then** (This means the learning period is over.)
15:     **if** $mean\ returns\_up \geq mean\ returns\_down$ **then**
16:         $current\_price \leftarrow current\_price + \epsilon$
17:         $returns\_up \leftarrow []$
18:         $returns\_down \leftarrow []$
19:     **else**
20:         $current\_price \leftarrow current\_price - \epsilon$
21:     **end if**
22: **end if**
23: Back to step 5

Table 1. Parameters used in simulation

	Value
γ	10
v	100
ϵ	0.7
δ	3
θ	3
Epoch length	30
Initial price	20
Firm costs	0
Number of firms	3

merging party will be 17.67, while the non-merged party will produce 28.71. Prices of the merged and non-merged parties will be very close, being 3.69 and 3.39 respectively.

In the Netlogo model, there are sliders that determine the value of learning parameters, such as ϵ and δ, demand parameters, such as γ and v, initial prices, firm costs, the number of firms (Fig. 1).

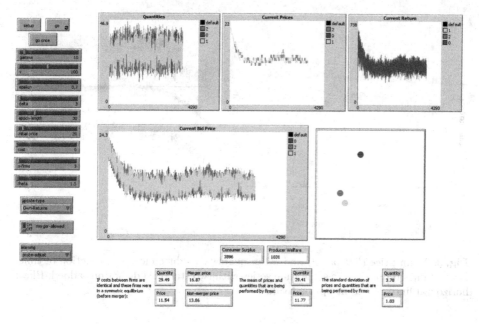

Fig. 1. Typical run in the model.

4   Results

In this section we will discuss the results of the model considering the parameters chosen for our simulations. First we will analyze results obtained before mergers and then after mergers. Finally, statistical tests will be run to compare means of current prices between each of the circumstances.

Before Mergers

As a first experiment, 10 runs with the given parameters were considered to understand the model's behavior. Every period (step), the mean and standard deviation of prices, quantities and welfare values were taken. The data was grouped by step, so notice that these are the average of means and standard deviations. Figure 2 shows the progression of prices and quantities as time evolves. In our simulations, the stability of prices occur around the 600*th* period.

At the optimum, considering symmetric prices, quantities should be around 29.49. The mean quantity produced by firms follows that very closely, as seen on the right panel of the Fig. 2. The mean current quantity is around 29.4 with a standard deviation of around 1.5. Regarding prices, the optimal price is 11.54. Firms in the model have a mean current price of 11.75, higher than the optimal price by a small number; the standard deviation of current prices is around 0.5.

Before mergers actually happen, after a learning period, optimal prices and quantities are achieved by firms. Naturally, the adjustment process depends on

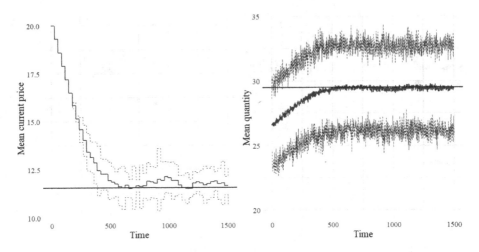

Fig. 2. Mean price (left panel) and mean quantity (right panel) as a function of time. Dashed lines represent the same time series with two standard deviations added. Black horizontal lines represent optimal values.

the learning parameters. For example, if $\epsilon = 2$, adjustment would happen around the $250th$ period. However, the standard deviations of prices and quantities would be higher. Consequently, an adjustment to the stability parameter (θ) would be necessary to consider the higher standard deviation[6].

After Mergers

The next experiment is related to the effect of mergers on prices. Once again, 10 runs with the given initial parameters were considered, but now mergers happen only starting at the $1500th$ period and the stability condition is achieved[7]. Immediate results are given in Fig. 3, which shows prices after a merger has taken place and involves two of the three companies. Increases in prices are present for both groups that are in the industry: the merged party and the non-merged. Following the analytical model, mean prices are around 16.5 with standard deviation of 1.08 for the merging party. In the case of the non-merging firm, mean price is 13.6 and its standard deviation is 0.724.

Because this difference in prices could be due to randomness, statistical tests were conducted to help decide if the difference in means are significant. The result from a one-way ANOVA[8] test suggests that the null hypothesis of equal price means between merged and non-merged parties can be rejected with a confidence level of 95%. When considering a non-parametric test, such as Kruskal-Wallis[9],

---

[6] This is relevant only when mergers are allowed.
[7] This means that firms merge around the 1590th period.
[8] See [4].
[9] See [7].

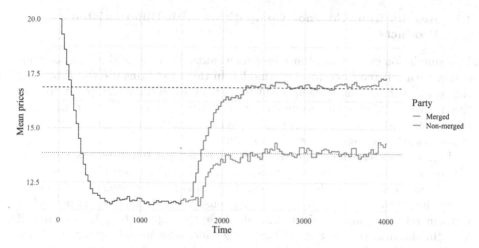

Fig. 3. Mean prices after a merger. Dashed lines represent optimal prices for each party after mergers.

the result is the same: we reject the null hypothesis that means are equal. This suggests the changes observed after a merger are not only by chance.

As suggested by the analytical model, a merger leads to an increase in prices for both parties in the market (the merged and the non-merged). If prices are increasing, consumer's and producer's surpluses are both affected. The left panel of Fig. 4 shows the evolution of surplus for both parties. Not only consumer surplus decreases after a merger, the total welfare, which is the sum of the surpluses for both parties, decreases as shown in the right panel. This is another expected result in the analytical model.

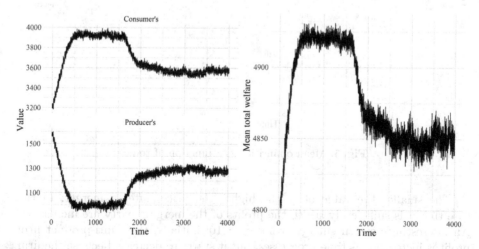

Fig. 4. Welfare measures time progression. The left panel shows the consumer's and welfare's surpluses, while the right panel shows total welfare.

4.1 Results from Cournot Competition with Differentiated Products

This simulation experiment considered an agentized version of the Cournot competion with differentiated products model. In this case, firms use the *Probe and Adjust* algorithm to define their quantities. Firms are initially engaged in competition and try to learn the optimal quantities, that is, quantities that maximize their profits. After the 1590*th* period, firms in the system merge and adjust their quantities considering the new arrangement.

Figure 5 shows the mean quantities chosen by firms in the system as a function of time. Initially, the mean quantities chosen by firms are higher than the Nash equilibrium, considering the chosen parameters. For that reason, quantities are decreasing until they're stable, which happens around the 600*th* period. When firms merge, the multi-product firms decrease their quantities. In response, if $\gamma = 10$, the firm that is outside the merger increases its sold quantity. When $\gamma = 2$, quantities for the merged firm decrease, but the firm that is not part of the merger does not increase its quantity as much. This is the predicted result in the analytical model, which attests the precision of the agent-based version, even when considering that firms are rationally bounded.

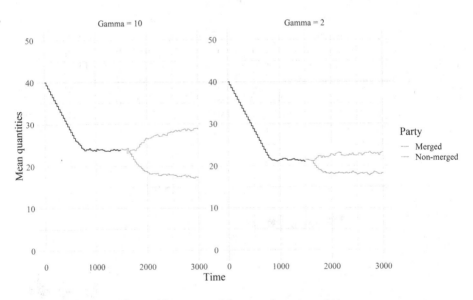

Fig. 5. Mean quantities as a function of time

The smaller the value of γ, the higher the prices after a merger. In the case that γ is sufficiently small, the profits of the merging party are increasing. An interesting pattern emerges when $\gamma = 10$: initially, the multi-product firm profit is increasing as time progresses, but it starts to decrease because the firm that is outside of the merger starts increasing its produced quantity. This is happening because the firm that is outside of the merger does not know that increasing quantities will lead to an increase in its profit. Finally, it's noticeable that mergers are unambiguously beneficial to the firm that is outside of the merger in the Cournot case. These results are observed in Fig. 6.

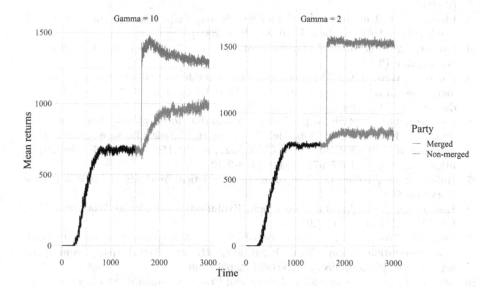

Fig. 6. Mean profits as a function of time

5   Concluding Remarks and Future Extensions

Our paper has shown how the agentization of a horizontal merger can be conducted considering firms with imperfect rationality and incomplete information. Even with a rudimentary method, such as the Probe and Adjust, in which firms are basically trying and guessing prices, firms can adapt to their environment and learn optimal prices and quantities in distinct scenarios: without and with mergers.

For future extensions of this work, alternative learning methods should be implemented and compared to the Probe and Adjust. Heterogeneous learning is an interesting extension to this work because different pricing patterns could emerge. For this future implementation, candidate methods could be the least squares method and the gradient learning. Another relevant extension to this work would be the inclusion of spatial competition: an additional parameter could be added to the utility function of the representative consumer in order to denote its preferences according to a firm's distance. Another way to explore spatial competition would be in the ways proposed by [9], in which consumers are uniformly distributed in a unit circle.

References

1. Berry, S., Levinsohn, J., Pakes, A.: Automobile prices in market equilibrium. Econometrica (1995)
2. DeSouza, S.A.: Antitrust mixed logit model. Série Estudos Econômicos (04), 4 (2009)
3. Epstein, R.J., Rubinfeld, D.: Merger simulation: a simplified approach with new applications. Antitrust Law J. **69**, 883–919 (2002)
4. Everitt, B., Hothorn, T.: A Handbook of Statistical Analyses Using R. CRC Press, Boca Raton (2009)
5. Froeb, L., Werden, G.: The effects of mergers in differentiated products industries: logit demand and merger policy. J Law Econ Organ **10**, 407–26 (1994). https://doi.org/10.1093/oxfordjournals.jleo.a036857
6. Guerrero, O.A., Axtell, R.L.: Using agentization for exploring firm and labor dynamics. In: Osinga, S., Hofstede, G., Verwaart, T. (eds.) Lecture Notes in Economics and Mathematical Systems, vol. 652, pp. 139–150. Springer, Berlin (2011). https://doi.org/10.1007/978-3-642-21108-9_12
7. Hollander, M., Wolfe, D.: Nonparametric Statistical Methods. John Wiley, New York (1973)
8. Kimbrough, S.O.: Agents, Games, and Evolution: Strategies at Work and Play. CRC Press, Boca Raton (2019)
9. Levy, D.T., Reitzes, J.D.: Anticompetitive effects of mergers in markets with localized competition. J. Law Econ. Organ. **8**(2), 427–40 (1992). https://EconPapers.repec.org/RePEc:oup:jleorg:v:8:y:1992:i:2:p:427-40
10. Motta, M.: Competition Policy: Theory and Practice. Cambridge University Press, Cambridge (2004)
11. Nardone, C.: Agent-based computational economics and industrial organization theory. In: Cecconi, F., Campennì, M. (eds.) Information and Communication Technologies (ICT) in Economic Modeling. CSS, pp. 3–14. Springer, Cham (2019). https://doi.org/10.1007/978-3-030-22605-3_1
12. Press, W.H., Teukolsky, S.A., Vetterling, W.T., Flannery, B.P.: Numerical Recipes 3rd Edition: The Art of Scientific Computing, 3rd edn. Cambridge University Press, Cambridge, USA (2007)
13. Railsback, S.F., Grimm, V.: Agent-Based and Individual-Based Modeling. Princeton University Press, Princêton (2019). https://www.ebook.de/de/product/34243950/steven_f_railsback_volker_grimm_agent_based_and_individual_based_modeling.html
14. Tesfatsion, L.: Chapter 16 agent-based computational economics: a constructive approach to economic theory. Handb. Comput. Econ. **2**, 831–880 (2006). https://doi.org/10.1016/S1574-0021(05)02016-2
15. Wilensky, U.: Netlogo (1999)

The Influence of National Culture on Evacuation Response Behaviour and Time: An Agent-Based Approach

Elvira Van Damme[1]([envelope])[iD], Natalie van der Wal[1][iD], Gert Jan Hofstede[2,3][iD], and Frances Brazier[1][iD]

[1] Faculty of Technology, Policy and Management, Delft University of Technology, Delft, The Netherlands
elviravandamme@hotmail.com, {c.n.vanderwal,f.m.brazier}@tudelft.nl
[2] Department of Social Sciences, Wageningen University and Research, Wageningen, The Netherlands
gertjan.hofstede@wur.nl
[3] Centre for Applied Risk Management, North-West University, Potchefstroom, South Africa

Abstract. "How does culture, in combination with cues, settings and affiliation, influence response-phase behaviour and time and total evacuation time?". A questionnaire and an agent-based model for a case study of a library evacuation in Czech Republic, Poland, Turkey and the UK have been developed to answer this question. Our questionnaire, conducted among 442 respondents (N = 105 from Czech Republic, N = 106 from Poland, N = 106 from Turkey and N = 125 from the United Kingdom), shows significant differences in the number of performed response tasks per culture - whereby Turkish respondents perform the most response tasks and British the least - and the results were directly implemented in our agent-based model. Simulation results show: (1) these differences - in combination with emergent effects for task choice and agent interactions - directly translate into the average response and evacuation times being highest for Turkey, followed by Poland, Czech Republic, and the UK, (2) cues, setting and affiliation influence response and evacuation time - such as being informed by staff giving a negative correlation and evacuating in groups a positive correlation with response time -, while the magnitude of these effects differ per culture. Our results suggest that faster response times might be related to dimensions of national culture, such as weak uncertainty avoidance and high individualism.

Keywords: Evacuation response behaviour · Agent-based model · Cross-cultural · Evacuation modelling

1 Introduction

The behaviour of building occupants is one of the most critical determinants for successful fire evacuations [10, 20]. The understanding of occupant behaviour can

F. Lorig and E. Norling (Eds.): MABS 2022, LNAI 13743, pp. 41–56, 2023.
https://doi.org/10.1007/978-3-031-22947-3_4

be used to make informed policy decisions, support emergency relief efforts and help with facilitating building design and developing public emergency education [15].

Building fire evacuation behaviour consists of two major phases: the response and the evacuation movement phase [8]. During the response phase, an occupant is notified of unusual happenings, after which an occupant performs tasks to validate what is happening and to prepare for evacuation movement. The response phase is followed by the evacuation movement phase, during which an occupant performs purposeful movement towards an exit or a place of safety.

Response phase tasks can be of two kinds. Action tasks "involves the occupant physically undertaking an activity such as: shutting down a work station; packing work items; moving to another location, etc." [7] and Information tasks "involves the occupant seeking, providing or exchanging information concerning the incident or required course of action." [7]. The duration of the response phase is referred to as the response time. While incident analyses have shown a connection between the response time and the number of fatalities [10], response-phase research has been frequently ignored or oversimplified [28]. The duration of the response phase and the evacuation movement phase together form the total evacuation time.

Three important factors influence response-phase behaviour: cues, setting, and affiliation [18]. A cue in this context is described as "a change in the environment indicating something wrong or different from usual" [25], setting refers to the location and surroundings of an occupant [21], while affiliation refers to people with whom an occupant is connected during the evacuation, such as family or friends [25].

Cues come from different sources: from the fire itself (flames, smoke), warning systems (alarm, light flashes) and other people (occupants, firefighters) [2]. Building occupants go through an extensive decision-making process in which they continuously receive different information from cues, process this information, solicit additional information if necessary, and take actions accordingly [16].

The types of cues an occupant receives are highly dependent upon the occupant's setting. The theory of occupancy [24], represents the setting as "the constraints on, conditions and possibilities of knowledge and actions afforded by the social, organisational and physical locations occupied by people over time" [21]. According to this theory, the setting may influence how an occupant behaves. Herein the social context plays a role. For example, an occupant will not be able to speak to others when there is no one around.

Besides the environmental setting of an occupant, affiliation is of influence. According to the theory of affiliation [25], people have the tendency to seek the familiar in uncertain situations, as they feel safer in a known environment. Many building occupants tend to seek their friends and relatives before starting evacuation, causing high delays [23].

Besides the cues, setting and affiliation, culture influences building fire behaviour [8,19]. Culture is defined as "the collective programming of the mind distinguishing the members of one group or category of people from others" [9]. Culture can be found anywhere and can be of multiple forms, from organisational cultures to cultures within social classes and cultures associated with religion [3]. For this study, culture is defined as national culture. As exposure to a new homeland could modify or override ones organic cultural influences [17], in this paper we focus on national culture: the culture of people with the same nationality, living in the same country. National culture can be described by Hofstede's six cultural dimensions: Power Distance, Individualism, Masculinity, Uncertainty Avoidance, Long Term Orientation and Indulgence [9]. For each of the dimensions, values can be allocated to a population to describe the norms and values and behaviour of that population. Out of a maximum score of 100, UK scores the lowest on uncertainty avoidance (35 for UK versus Czech Republic (74), Turkey (85) and Poland (93)), but the highest on Individualism (89 for UK versus Czech Republic (58), Poland (60) and Turkey (37) [9]). Most evacuation research is executed for countries with similar cultural backgrounds: UK, USA, Canada, Australia and New Zealand [7]. There is little research available on the effect of culture on evacuation behaviour for other countries, nor is there data available. Due to this lack of research, the same evacuation data is frequently used to provide evacuation insights within very different cultures [7]. However, findings from one country cannot be applied directly to others, as the few cross-cultural studies performed, have shown significant influences of culture on evacuation behaviour. Cross-cultural studies have shown how culture influences levels of emotions during an evacuation [1] and tendencies to evacuate [13]. Furthermore, studies have shown how culture influences personal space [22] and walking speed [14]. Additionally, the BeSeCu project [7], found that culture influences the number of tasks performed during the response phase of an evacuation. During this project, 4 unannounced evacuation drills took place in Czech Republic, Poland, Turkey and the UK. This project measured the number of response tasks performed, as well as the response and evacuation times. However, the project did not take into account the types of response tasks performed and their interactions with other influential factors. This inspired us for the setup of our study.

As culture, cues, setting and affiliation have been shown to influence response-phase behaviour [7,18], our study explores the potential effects of their interactions on response-phase behaviour and response and evacuation time. Therefore, our main research question is: "How does culture, in combination with cues, settings and affiliation, influence response time and total evacuation time?".

To answer the research question, an agent-based model has been developed based on a case study on library evacuation in Czech Republic, Poland, Turkey and the UK [7], together with literature research and knowledge acquired through a questionnaire administered (online) in each of these countries. Our questionnaire results - type and order of response phase tasks - have been directly translated into model input, to simulate detailed evacuation behaviours of library visitors during a fire incident. The behaviour of library staff is considered to be culture-independent, as staff behaviour could be largely affected by the types of training that they have had [5].

The rest of this paper is organised as follows. Section 2 addresses the questionnaire results and the model setup. Section 3 shows the model results. Section 4 discusses the results, strengths, weaknesses, implications, future research and ends with a conclusion.

2   Methods

Empirical evacuation experiments are often costly and labour intensive. This paper takes an agent-based modelling and simulation approach with the aim to understand response phase behaviours themselves and their effects on response and evacuation time. Agent-based models provide the ability to implement social structures and to capture emergent phenomena. The input of our model and the agent behaviours modelled are based on a literature review and our questionnaire study results [26], summarised below. Then, the model is explained.

2.1   Case Study Contextualisation

As described above, the case-study considers four national cultures: Czech Republic, Poland, Turkey and the UK. A library evacuation is chosen as this situation is considered to be similar for all countries. First of all, library buildings in the four countries are expected to be similar and building occupants are expected to have similar demographics. Furthermore the types of activities performed in the libraries are of a similar nature.

The case-study considers a fire in the library. All staff members and visitors hear a fire alarm. This alarm contains a voice message announcing an emergency in the building and that everyone needs to leave the building. This is followed by an alarm tone. The cues, setting and affiliation that can influence the situation and behaviour of the building visitors are described in Table 1.

2.2   Questionnaire Results Used for Model Input and Agent Behaviours

A total of 20 response tasks (9 information and 11 action tasks) were identified for a library evacuation on the basis of a literature review [26], see Table 2. Participants were asked which tasks and in which order they would perform these tasks for a series of scenarios; within which cues, setting and affiliation also played a role. The questionnaire was translated into the native languages of the respondents. The inclusion criteria for the respondents were: age (18–40 years old), their residency and nationality (both from the same country), and experience with visiting a public library at least once.

Table 1. Implementation of culture, cues, setting and affiliation

Influential factor	Implementation
Culture	National culture implemented through 4 countries: Czech Republic, Poland, Turkey and the UK.
Cues (2 types)	(1) Being informed by a staff member: A staff member tells a visitor that there is an emergency and that the visitor needs to leave the building as quickly as possible. (2) Seeing signs of fire and/or smoke.
Setting	Being surrounded by others (anyone present within a distance of 20 m) or being in a closed off space/not nearby others.
Affiliation	Small groups of two coworkers/friends present in the building. These two people can be together or separated in space at any point in time.

Data analysis was performed for 442 participants (217 females; 220 males; 5 other), with N = 105 from Czech Republic, N = 106 from Poland, N = 106 from Turkey and N = 125 from the United Kingdom. The main results include significant differences in the total number of tasks reported, this was found by performing a one-way ANOVA test (F(3.416) = 8.888; p = 0.000). Respondents from Turkey perform the highest number of tasks (M = 5.42, SD = 2.82), followed in decreasing order by Poland (M = 5.05, SD = 2.08), Czech Republic (M = 4.54, SD = 2.18), and the UK (M = 3.86, SD = 2.14). Secondly, the study showed that more information tasks than action tasks are reported for all countries. Thirdly, response behaviour in all countries is shown to be influenced by cues, setting and affiliation, as these influence the number of tasks performed and the types of tasks performed. The influence of the cues, setting and affiliation on response behaviour differs per country [26]. For example, probabilities

Table 2. Identified information and action tasks in a library situation [26]

Information tasks	Action tasks
Phone someone to seek information	Shut down workstation, lock files, tidy desk etc.
Engage with electronic media to seek information	Pack personal and work items in close vicinity
Seek information through conversations with other people nearby	Collect and put on coat
Move to another location to seek information	Change footwear/glasses/clothing
Look around and listen to what is happening	Physically assist others
Seek information through professional bodies	Collect emergency equipment
Phone someone to provide information	Move to another location to collect personal/work items
Actively provide information and/or instructions to others nearby	Move to another location to find friends/coworkers
Actively search for others in the building, to inform them	Wait for a friend/coworker to leave
	Call alarm number
	Fight fire

for collecting belongings decreases after seeing fire, however these probabilities decrease with 21% for the UK, while these decrease with only 10% for Poland.

2.3 Agent-Based Evacuation Model Including National Cultures

An agent-based model was designed and implemented in NetLogo as follows.

Agents. The model consists of two types of agents: visitors and staff members of a library. Visitors are people who do not perform official work at the library and staff members are people who do perform work in the library on a regular basis. Visitors and staff members perform different behaviours based on the rule-role model [6]. Staff members all perform similar behaviour for each culture, as the behaviour of library staff could be largely affected by the types of training that they have had [5]. The behaviour of the visitors is culture dependent in line with [26].

Environment. A library was chosen as a common environment inspired by [7]. The model represents a two-dimensional space, based on a floor plan from the ground floor of Delft University of Technology's Library, see Fig. 1. In NetLogo, the floor plan consists of 200 by 190 patches, with each patch representing an area of 2 by 2 m.

The patches are coloured in one of seven colours, with each colour representing specific characteristics. *Black* patches represent walls inside the building or areas outside the building. These patches are not accessible by agents. *Red* patches represent exits of the building. *Blue* patches indicate areas where sitting places are located. *Lilac* patches indicate areas which are closed offices, in which only one person can sit at a time. *Orange and yellow* indicate fire. Patches only

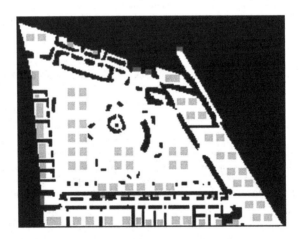

Fig. 1. Floor plan of the TU Delft library as used in the model

colour orange or yellow, whenever a fire occurred within the building. As this area is dangerous, agents are not able to access these patches. Finally, *White* patches represent all other patches inside the building, that are not represented by any of the colours above.

Evacuation Behaviour. All of the building occupants go through the following four phases: Normal phase, Response phase, Evacuating phase and Evacuated phase. During the Normal phase, agents are not aware of any unusual happenings. During the Response phase, agents receive the first cues of the fire and search for information and prepare for evacuation. The agents perform purposeful movement towards an exit during the Evacuating phase and they reach the Evacuated phase whenever they have reached an exit in the library. Additionally, agents interact with their environments through communication with visitors and staff members, through observations and avoidance of fire, obstacles and other agents, through signals of a fire alarm and connections with friends and/or colleagues. As the focus of this research is on the Response phase, cultural aspects are considered in this phase only.

Response Phase Behaviour. Generally, three methodologies can be identified for simulating occupant behaviour during the response phase [12]. One method is to assign a time of delay to account for any actions that might be performed during the response phase by an individual, occupants remain stationary in their position, until they start moving towards an exit [11]. In the second method, building occupants are assigned a specific behavioural itinerary or a specific task. A specific time has been assigned for performing each of these tasks. The building occupant performs his/her itinerary actions, before starting the evacuation movement. The third method uses a predictive-style model, where one particular type of cue influences a particular type of evacuation behaviour. Examples of such cue-behaviour linkages are: presence of exit signage leading to choice of a specific evacuation route and smoke obscuration level influencing exit choices [11].

In our model, the second and third method are combined. The occupants have an itinerary and execute these tasks, however, cues and affiliation cause adjustments in the itinerary. The process is shown in Fig. 2.

The response phase decision-making of a visitor consists of three parts: the initial response tasks, adjustment of response tasks due to cues and setting and finalising response tasks. Visitors execute all of their itinerary tasks in the given sequence until they are all finished. Whenever another occupant approaches them to ask something or provide information, they will pause performance of their tasks for the time duration of this conversation. For the model, all 20 response tasks have been modelled separately and in detail. For example, for the task "Seek information through professional bodies" (depicted in Fig. 3), a visitor will look/walk around to see if there is a staff member nearby. If there is a staff member nearby, the visitor will walk towards the staff member. They will both remain together for a few seconds, during which the staff member will inform

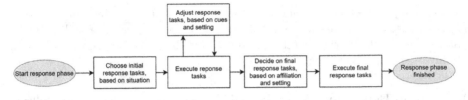

Fig. 2. Response phase decision-making of visitors

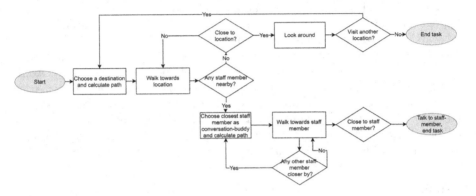

Fig. 3. Process "Seek information through professional bodies"

the visitor to evacuate as quickly as possible. Afterwards, they both continue with the rest of their itinerary.

A visitor's initial response itinerary is dependent on the cues received before the start of the response phase and the setting. Two types of cues are considered: signs of smoke or fire and being informed by a staff member. The setting can be either one in which there are other occupants in nearby surroundings or one in which there are not. By combining these cues and settings, multiple situations arise. For each situation, a probability tree developed based on the questionnaire data, determines the response itinerary to be performed. The probability trees indicate probabilities for which tasks are to be performed in which sequence. Through randomisation, an initial itinerary for the visitor will be selected from the probability tree.

Different factors can influence execution of a building occupant's itinerary. Firstly, the two types of cues involved are of influence: signs of smoke and/or fire and being informed by a staff member. The questionnaire data is used to alter the tasks not executed yet. This means that there are certain chances that an occupant may remove tasks from his/her itinerary or that new tasks, not initially included in the itinerary, will be added to the itinerary. Additionally, the setting influences an agent's choice to perform tasks related to location. For example, when the itinerary states that an occupant will collect his/her coat, the choice to do so may depend on the location of the agent. An extra decision process on whether to move to the location or not may be needed if the coat is not close to the occupant.

After finalising the previously defined itinerary, there is a possibility that more tasks will be added. Firstly, if a building occupant has not executed any tasks concerning his/her belongings, there is a possibility to pick these up after finishing all tasks. Secondly, if a building occupant is in the library together with a friend or colleague, he/she must decide to search/wait for this friend, or not.

After all response tasks have been finished, the Evacuation phase starts. The full model and model overview can be downloaded from GitHub [27].

2.4 Model Validation

The model results were validated against the empirical results of the BeSeCu project [7], figures used for the comparison can be found in [27].

The comparison of our model results and the empirical BeSeCu results [7] show similar patterns for the response time distributions and the number of people evacuated over time. However, different orders of magnitude for the response and evacuation times were detected. This can be explained by the following two reasons. Firstly, participants in the BeSeCu project could repeat response tasks, while in our model this was not possible as repetitions could not be measured by the questionnaire software used. Secondly, our model uses similar notification times for all countries, as there is limited information available on cultural influences on notification times. For the BeSeCu project, however, the notification times differed per country. As it was not possible to validate the model with data other than that of the BeSeCu project [7], the obtained results should only be used within the context of this study. The overall model behaviour and the effect of influential factors do seem to align; however the exact quantitative outcomes have not been validated.

3 Results

3.1 Effects of Culture on Response and Total Evacuation Time

Figure 4 shows how the total evacuation times per country are made up of notification time, time used to perform response tasks and time used for evacuation movement. The response tasks take up most of the evacuation time (201–278 s), followed by movement time (150–156 s) and notification time (43–44 s). Interestingly, Czech Republic, Poland, Turkey and the UK differ on the response tasks time, while notification times are quite similar for all four countries. This indicates that differences between the countries in emergent response behaviour do not affect notification times.

The plots in Fig. 5, show response and evacuation time distributions per country. The average response time is highest in Turkey ($M = 290.79$, $SD = 24.27$), followed by Poland ($M = 262.79$, $SD = 20.48$), Czech Republic ($M = 234.80$, $SD = 14.39$) and the UK ($M = 214.02$, $SD = 34.63$). These times differ due to the

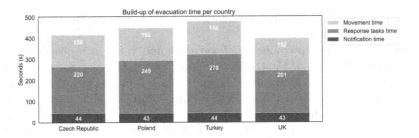

Fig. 4. Build-up of total evacuation time per culture

number of tasks performed per country and the types of tasks performed. Similarly, the average evacuation time is highest in Turkey (M = 416.79, SD = 28.98), followed by Poland (M = 385.13, SD = 29.93), Czech Republic (M = 355.60, SD = 15.37) and the UK (M = 336.39, SD = 19.90). One-way ANOVA analyses and post-hoc tests show significant differences for both response and evacuation times, between each of the four countries. These distributions relate to the model input for the total number of tasks performed. The UK performs fewer, and Turkey performs more, tasks than the other countries. Additionally, a larger spread for the number of tasks in Turkey was found compared to the Czech Republic, Poland, and the UK. This is directly translated into the response times.

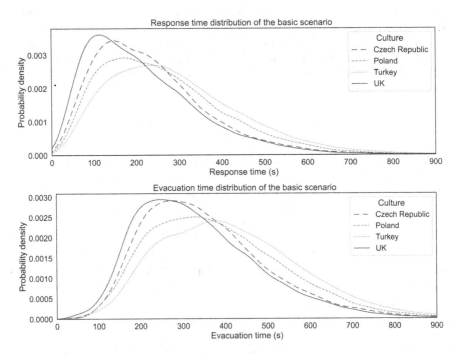

Fig. 5. Distributions of the response and evacuation times of all visitors

3.2 Effect of Cues, Setting and Affiliation on Response and Total Evacuation Time

Two cues were analysed: being informed by a staff member or seeing fire or smoke. Two settings were analysed: how does the chance of being in a closed off space/not around others influence the outcome? For affiliation, the number of friend/colleague groups in the building have been analysed. Correlations have been calculated for each influential factor (cue, setting, affiliation) in combination with each of the model outcomes (average response and evacuation time). Pearson's r correlation tests have been used to find out if these observed correlations are significant. An overview of all correlations is depicted in Table 3.

Table 3. Correlations between influential factors (cues, setting, affiliation) and model outcomes (average response or evacuation time) for each of the four countries (Czech Republic, Poland, Turkey, UK).

Influencing factor	Pearson r correlations between influencing factor and outcome variable			
	Czech Rep.	Poland	Turkey	UK
Model outcome: average response time				
Cue: Informed by staff	−0.5755**	−0.4820**	−0.4007**	−0.4365**
Cue: Fire Seen	0.2944**	0.2213**	0.2148**	0.1439*
Affiliation	0.7739**	0.7363**	0.7044**	0.7528**
Setting	0.1678**	0.0872	0.1034	0.1318*
Model outcome: average evacuation time				
Cue: Informed by staff	−0.5713**	−0.5326**	−0.4391**	−0.4744**
Cue: Fire Seen	0.2463**	0.2074**	0.2436**	0.1400
Affiliation	0.7058**	0.6862**	0.7034**	0.6946**
Setting	0.1356*	0.0581	0.1116*	0.1644**

Note. Significance: * $p \leq 0.05$, ** $p \leq 0.01$

Cues. A negative correlation has been found between average response time and the percentage of people informed: average response times decrease as the percentage of people informed increases, see Fig. 7. This effect is highest for Czech Republic ($r = -0.58$, $p \leq 0.01$) and lowest for Turkey ($r = -0.4$, $p \leq 0.01$). These differences can be traced back to the model input, in which the Czech Republic has shown the highest decrease in the number of response tasks reported after being informed by a staff member. A similar influence of the cue on the average evacuation time is found. While the correlation stays the same for Czech Republic, there are slight increases for each of the other countries. This effect can be explained by a positive relationship that was found between the number of staff members in the building and the percentage of visitors informed by a staff member. This effect levels out whenever the number of staff members in the building increases and a high percentage of the visitors is informed.

Response times slightly increase, for all countries, if more people have seen fire, see Fig. 6. This effect is highest for Czech Republic ($r = 0.29$, $p \leq 0.01$) and lowest for the UK ($r = 0.14$, $p \leq 0.05$). The cause of these higher response times cannot be traced back to the number of tasks performed after seeing the fire, to affiliative behaviour or to the collection of belongings. Therefore, it seems caused by changes in the types of tasks performed. All countries report a relatively high likelihood of calling the emergency number or fighting the fire. Both of these tasks take up a relatively large amount of time.

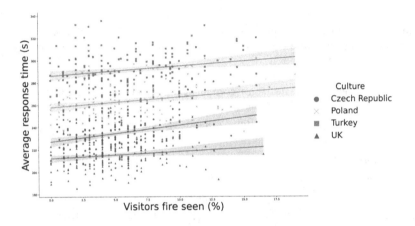

Fig. 6. The effect of seeing fire on average response time

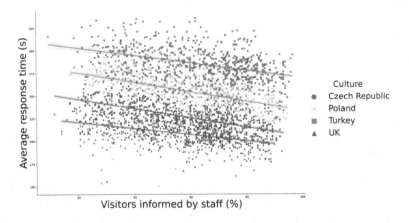

Fig. 7. The effect of being informed by a staff member on average response time

Setting. Small positive correlations between the setting and the average response time were found for Czech Republic ($r = 0.17$, $p \leq 0.01$) and the UK ($r = 0.13$, $p \leq 0.05$), while for Poland and Turkey, no significant correlations were found. What is noticeable, is how the response times differ less when 25 visitors are inside the building in comparison to more people inside the building.

It was expected that response times would decrease whenever more people are present in the building, because chances of being informed by another visitor, or seeing others evacuate, increase. However, this effect was not found thus it seems that the effects of the setting can be explained by clogging and the possibility to perform more response tasks.

Affiliation. Response times in Czech Republic, Poland, Turkey and the UK are all strongly influenced by affiliation. Response times increase whenever there are more friend groups in the building. Czech Republic is most influenced by this parameter ($r = 0.77$, $p \leq 0.01$) and Turkey the least influenced ($r = 0.70$, $p \leq 0.01$). The high effect on Czech visitors is related to the likelihood of showing affiliative behaviour, as found in the questionnaire. Similar are observable for the effect of affiliation on the average evacuation time.

4   Discussion and Conclusion

This study answered the following research question: *"How does culture, in combination with cues, settings and affiliation, influence response-phase behaviour and time and total evacuation time?"*.

The main finding is that the countries all have significantly different response and evacuation times. Simulation results indicate that Turkey is slowest during both the response phase and the total evacuation. This is followed by Poland, Czech Republic, and the UK. This order is similar to the order of the number of tasks reported in the questionnaire. It thus seems to be a direct result of the behavioural input (number of response tasks) used for the model in combination with emergent effects due to task choice and agent interactions, such as staff warning visitors and visitors evacuating in small groups. Combining the findings of the questionnaire and model shows that higher number of response tasks seem to lead to higher response times and total evacuation time. This corresponds with other evacuation research [4], that found that an increased number of tasks contributes to an increased response time. The model outcomes and the effect of different factors (cues, setting, affiliation) on the model outcomes seem valid at the level of "stylized facts". Exact quantitative outcomes have not been validated, and would not be expected to correspond, due to simplifications inherent in modelling. Although there were differences in the number of tasks performed and the notification times used in the BeSeCu project [7], the overall patterns in the response time distribution and the people evacuated over time generated by our model were similar to those of these empirical experiments.

The differences in response behaviours among the countries, found in the survey and simulation results, could be related with Hofstede's cultural dimension scores, however these are conjectures at this moment, as yet not confirmed by empirical research. We speculate that UK showing the fastest response times might relate to the lower score on uncertainty avoidance and higher score on individualism versus the other three countries. According to [9], cultures with a high uncertainty avoidance tend to get more anxious in ambiguous situations. Our interpretation is that a weak uncertainty avoidance leads to performing less information tasks, and thus a faster response time for the UK versus the other countries. In individualist societies, people are expected to take care of themselves and not necessarily of the larger group [9]. We speculate that individualistic cultures might be less inclined to use communication or information gains during an evacuation, leading to faster response times for the UK, versus the other countries. Briefly said, a Brit is more likely to just go for it. Additionally, we speculate that collectivist cultures (of which Turkey is an example in our sample), are more likely to perform affiliative behaviour, which causes slower response times. A strength of this research is in the detail of the analysis in how response behaviour is influenced by cultures and how these cultural behaviours are affected by cues, setting and affiliation. No previous studies have combined these two aspects and especially not in as much detail as in this study. Additionally, the agent based model developed for this study is based on behavioural data, making the outcomes more powerful and reliable compared to other studies. This model could be applied to other environments, but also to other cultures and to include other factors that influence the Response phase.

Limitations of this research can be found in the simplification of evacuation behaviour, the method to collect behavioural data through a questionnaire and the limited knowledge available for modelling response tasks. Future research can cope with these limitations by extending this research with other factors that influence behaviour, conducting empirical evacuation experiments, and studying what behaviour is performed exactly during the different task types. Furthermore, future research poses opportunities for studying response behaviour in other cultures and environments, studying environments with mixed cultures and developing adequate evacuation policies.

Overall, this research provides a new approach and an agent-based model to study the effect of cultures, in combination with cues, setting and affiliation, on response-phase behaviour and response and evacuation times. Acknowledging the importance of cross-cultural research for evacuation behaviour adds value for policy makers and emergency planners. This research can be used as a starting point for discussions among safety practitioners and other stakeholders.

References

1. Almejmaj, M., Skorinko, J.L., Meacham, B.J.: The effects of cultural differences between the us and Saudi Arabia on emergency evacuation-analysis of self reported recogntion/reaction times and cognitive state. Case Stud. Fire Saf. **7**, 1–7 (2016). https://doi.org/10.1016/j.csfs.2016.12.002
2. Brennan, P.: Modelling cue recognition and pre-evacuation response. Fire Saf. Sci. **6**, 1029–1040 (2000). https://doi.org/10.3801/IAFSS.FSS.6-1029

3. Cohen, A.B.: Many forms of culture. Am. Psychol. **64**(3), 194–204 (2009). https://doi.org/10.1037/a0015308
4. Day, R.C., Hulse, L.M., Galea, E.R.: Response phase behaviours and response time predictors of the 9/11 world trade center evacuation. Fire Technol. **49**(3), 657–678 (2013). https://doi.org/10.1007/s10694-012-0282-9
5. Formolo, D., Bosse, T., van der Wal, N.: Studying the impact of trained staff on evacuation scenarios by agent-based simulation. In: Staab, S., Koltsova, O., Ignatov, D.I. (eds.) SocInfo 2018. LNCS, vol. 11186, pp. 85–96. Springer, Cham (2018). https://doi.org/10.1007/978-3-030-01159-8_8
6. Fridolf, K., Nilsson, D., Frantzich, H.: Fire evacuation in underground transportation systems: a review of accidents and empirical research. Fire Technol. **49**(2), 451–475 (2013). https://doi.org/10.1007/s10694-011-0217-x
7. Galea, E.R., Markus, S., Deere, S.J., Filippidis, L.: Investigating the impact of culture on evacuation response behaviour (2015)
8. Galea, E., Sharp, G., Deere, S., Filippidis, L.: Investigating the impact of culture on evacuation behavior - a Turkish data-set, vol. 10 (2012). https://doi.org/10.3801/IAFFS.FSS.10-709
9. Hofstede, G., Hofstede, G.J., Minkov, M.: Cultures and Organizations - Software of the Mind: Intercultural Cooperation and its Importance for Survival, 3rd edn. McGraw-Hill, New York (2010)
10. Kobes, M., Helsloot, I., Vries, D., Post, J.: Building safety and human behaviour in fire: a literature review. Fire Saf. J. **45**, 1–11 (2010). https://doi.org/10.1016/j.firesaf.2009.08.005
11. Kuligowski, E.: Predicting human behavior during fires. Fire Technol. **49**(1), 101–120 (2013). https://doi.org/10.1007/s10694-011-0245-6
12. Kuligowski, E.D., Peacock, R.D., Hoskins, B.L.: A Review of Building Evacuation Models; 2nd Edition. NIST Technical Note 1680, p. 36 (2010)
13. Lazo, J.K., Bostrom, A., Morss, R.E., Demuth, J.L., Lazrus, H.: Factors affecting hurricane evacuation intentions. Risk Anal. **35**(10), 1837–1857 (2015). https://doi.org/10.1111/risa.12407
14. Levine, R., Norenzayan, A.: The pace of life in 31 countries. J. Cross-cult. Psychol. **30**, 178–205 (1999). https://doi.org/10.1177/0022022199030002003
15. Lin, J., Zhu, R., Li, N., Becerik-Gerber, B.: Do people follow the crowd in building emergency evacuation? A cross-cultural immersive virtual reality-based study. Adv. Eng. Inf. **43**, 101040 (2020). https://doi.org/10.1016/j.aei.2020.101040
16. Lindell, M.K., Perry, R.W.: The protective action decision model: theoretical modifications and additional evidence. Risk Anal. **32**(4), 616–632 (2012). https://doi.org/10.1111/j.1539-6924.2011.01647.x
17. Litvin, S.: Cross-cultural research: are researchers better served by knowing respondents' country of birth, residence, or citizenship? J. Travel Res. **42**, 186–190 (2003). https://doi.org/10.1177/0047287503254955
18. Liu, Y., Zhang, Z., Mao, Z.: Analysis of influencing factors in pre-evacuation time using interpretive structural modeling. Saf. Sci. **128**, 104785 (2020). https://doi.org/10.1016/j.ssci.2020.104785
19. Matsumoto, D.: Culture, context, and behavior. J. Pers. **75**(6), 1285–1320 (2007). https://doi.org/10.1111/j.1467-6494.2007.00476.x
20. Pan, X., Han, C.S., Dauber, K., Law, K.H.: Human and social behavior in computational modeling and analysis of egress. Autom. Constr. **15**, 448–461 (2006). https://doi.org/10.1016/j.autcon.2005.06.006

21. Samochine, D.A., Boyce, K., Shields, J.: An investigation into staff behaviour in unannounced evacuations of retail stores - implications for training and fire safety engineering. In: Fire Safety Science, pp. 519–530 (2005).https://doi.org/10.3801/IAFSS.FSS.8-519

22. Samovar, L., Porter, R., McDaniel, E., Roy, C.: Communication Between Cultures. Cengage Learning, Boston (2016)

23. Sime, J.: Movement toward the familiar. Environ. Behav. **17**, 697–724 (1985)

24. Sime, J.: Understanding human behaviour in fires-an emerging theory of occupancy. University of Ulster Faculty of Engineering, School of the Built Environment, Fire Safety Engineering Research and Technology Marks and Spencer Guest Lecture, Ulster (1999)

25. Sime, J.D.: Affiliative behaviour during escape to building exits. J. Environ. Psychol. **3**(1), 21–41 (1983). https://doi.org/10.1016/S0272-4944(83)80019-X

26. Van Damme, E.R.I., van der Wal, C.N., Galea, E., Minkov, M.: Unpublished manuscript: the effect of national culture on evacuation task behaviour: a cross-cultural survey (2022)

27. Van Damme, E.: The influence of culture on evacuation response task behaviour: data and model (2021). https://github.com/elviravandamme/EvacuationResponseCulture

28. Vistnes, J., Grubits, S.J., He, Y.: A Stochastic approach to occupant pre-movement in fires. In: Fire Safety Science, pp. 531–542 (2005). https://doi.org/10.3801/IAFSS.FSS.8-531

Simulating Work Teams Using MBTI Agents

Luiz Fernando Braz[1]([⊠])(ID), Cristina Maria D. Antona Bachert[2](ID),
and Jaime Simão Sichman[1](ID)

[1] Universidade de São Paulo, São Paulo, Brazil
{luiz.braz,jaime.sichman}@usp.br
[2] Universidade de Sorocaba, Sorocaba, Brazil
cristina.bachert@prof.uniso.br

Abstract. The study of human behavior in organizational environments
has been the focus of researchers who seek to identify factors that may
influence high-performance team building. In this context, agent-based
simulations have been used to model artificial agents with human personality profiles based on the MBTI model. This work aimed to investigate
whether MBTI personality types and different scenarios could influence
the teams' outcomes, observing how agents' behaviors might impact the
overall group performance. The results demonstrated that the scenario
can decisively impact agent teams' performance, and certain personality
type characteristics also influence these results.

Keywords: Multi-agent systems · MBTI · BDI · Human behavior

1 Introduction

The use of multi-agent systems to simulate human behavior has allowed a significant evolution in the study of human relationships in work environments [3–5].
The BDI architecture, which allows representing the decision-making process in
agents, has enabled significant advances in understanding the influence of specific human characteristics on decisions taken in contexts such as work. In this
sense, the MBTI [17] created from Carl Jungs' theory of personality types has
stood out as an important instrument for a better understanding of peoples'
characteristics and preferences in different situations.

In this work, we seek to explore the development of artificial agents that represent the various personality types described by MBTI theory, using studies [3–
5,21–23] considering different scenarios that demonstrate the creation of multi-
agent systems based on Myers and Briggs' model. The purpose is to observe
how different personalities could influence the performance of agent teams that
have common goals and are formed with different personality compositions, thus
advancing in the better understanding of characteristics that could decisively
impact on teams performance. The paper is organized as follows: in Sect. 2, we
describe the MBTI and its relationship with the high-performance team building.

© The Author(s), under exclusive license to Springer Nature Switzerland AG 2023
F. Lorig and E. Norling (Eds.): MABS 2022, LNAI 13743, pp. 57–69, 2023.
https://doi.org/10.1007/978-3-031-22947-3_5

Section 3 discusses the use of multi-agent systems to simulate the groups of agents with personalities presenting a model proposal considering closer situations to what we see in similar situations experienced in organizational context. In this section, we also present the formulation of the hypotheses that will be tested. Section 4 describes the research methodology and results of the experiments carried out. Section 5 is dedicated to discussing the results obtained, addressing future works, and commenting on the limitations of the current study.

2   MBTI and High Performance Teams

The Myers Briggs Type Indicator (MBTI) is a personality inventory that allows identifying a set of characteristics a person uses in spontaneous and comfortable way to act in their daily life [17]. It is a widely used as a self-knowledge resource because it allows recognition of talents and skills. These skills, in turn, could be strengthened or modified aiming at personal improvement [16]. Based on Jungs' theory, Myers and Briggs classified the typical attitudes of an individual, randomly distributed in the general population [13] in four dimensions, represented by dichotomies, which can often be observed in people, regardless of cultural or social factors.

We will use the same type of description adopted in previous studies [3–5], considering that the prevalence of one dichotomy pole in each of the four dimensions indicates the person's preferred mode of living. In this sense, the sixteen personality types defined by the MBTI are based on the following factors:

Extraversion (E) - Introversion (I) In this first dichotomy, it is seen that Extraverted individuals tend to act faster based on the external world using more evident and superficial information. They feel comfortable and confident even in unfamiliar environments. Introverts are the opposite. They use their ideas, personal values, and thoughts to define how to act, demonstrating a slower and more cautious reaction due to their reflective attitude. They prefer quieter environments and forms of communication that allow less direct contact with others.

Sensing (S) - Intuition (N) This dichotomy involves the perception and processing of information. The Sensing (S) type tends to be more focused on measurable and tangible data, which often allows them to make practical and pragmatic perceptions. While the Intuition (N) type relies on understanding the big picture seeking new possibilities with the information they have.

Thinking (T) - Feeling (F) This dichotomy leads with the decision-making process. Thinking (T) type individuals tend to make more impersonal decisions, based on socially valued principles and rules. In contrast, we can notice in Feeling (F) type individuals that decisions are based on empathy and conflict avoidance in interpersonal relationships.

Judgment (J) - Perceiving (P) Finally, the last dichotomy involves the way a person deals with everyday situations, including unforeseen events and routine changes. Judging (J) type people feel more comfortable acting from previously defined goals and planned actions in a methodical and organized way. While those with Perceiving (P) type are more flexible and agile in dealing with unforeseen circumstances. In these moments, instead of focusing on difficulties, they seek positive points and opportunities that can replace the original plan. Due to this more open attitude, they tend to have difficulties planning actions in a more organized way.

Each psychological type can be recognized as a personal way of acting in each of the instances defined here and can be identified early on life. The more frequently used skills tend to become dominant - however the arrangement is not permanent and can be intentionally modified based on environmental demands perceived by the individual. The changing indicates a person's better adaptation [13] to the environment, and it could be understood as a performance improvement based on the development of skills and talents [18].

Considering the urgent need to compose and strengthen high-performance teams, the use of MBTI in the organizational context allows professionals to identify and understand the influence that certain characteristics of their personality can have on their work. It is also useful to identify learning needs and choose strategies that can be more effective to improve skills, knowledge, and attitudes [31] that facilitate their performance in an unstable, complex, competitive, and constantly changing environment [24].

Hence the importance of using the MBTI to build and develop teamwork skills with self-knowledge goals. This tool allows a better understanding of the influence that certain personality qualities can have on the way each person performs their duties and interacts with teammates [24]. Although important, a persons' personality type is not a crucial factor in their professional success. Studies indicates that market conditions, available technology and organizational climate are factors that can overcome individual characteristics [11], making it difficult to adapt working conditions to the employees' psychological type [31].

3   Using an Agent-Based Approach to Simulate Work Teams

Multi-agent systems (MASs) have been widely used to study individual human behavior through computer simulations [27]. Autonomous agents, having their own independent existence, are conceived to represent entities capable of carrying out a particular process and interacting with other agents. The objective of multi-agent systems is to conceive the means to ensure that these agents want to cooperate and effectively do so in order to solve specific problems as soon as they are presented to the system [1].

The representation of rational behavior, in which the production of actions that further the goals of an agent, based upon their conception of the world, has been receiving attention from researchers, who seek means to describe, through the use of Artificial Intelligence techniques, the rational human behavior [2]. In this sense, the BDI (Belief-Desire-Intention) architecture has played an essential role in developing intelligent artificial agents to represent complex reasoning [19,28] possessing capabilities to take decisions in complex dynamic environments [20].

3.1   BDI Model Proposal

Some studies were carried out using the BDI architecture as a basis for modeling multi-agent systems [3–5, 21–23]. In these, the authors modeled agents with behaviors derived from concepts seen in the MBTI theory, in which they sought to extend the BDI architecture by representing in the agents the different types of personalities described in the MBTI.

In a first approach the authors [21–23] model agents containing functions that define how the BDI process can influence their behavior and decisions. In this model, the agent first senses the environment through a perception function receiving input values (e.g., distance to other agents). After that, the agent interprets these data in the context of their personality type preferences, thus formulating their beliefs. The agent then evaluates its beliefs defining its desires, taking into account its internal state, short- and long-term goals, and personality type. Finally, with its defined desires and attainable goals, the agent evaluates the best decision to make by converting its desires into intentions [4, 21].

In a second perspective [3–5] that we will also use in this work, it sought to adapt and extend the framework proposed by Salvit and Sklar to cover a broader scope considering a scenario closer to organizational realities. In addition, adaptations were proposed in the decision-making process of agents considering the use of multi-attribute decision making (MADM) [25] so that agents can evaluate different alternatives and rank them according to prioritization criteria adjusted following the MBTI theory [3].

In this proposal, multiple attributes are used to define the behavioral preferences of the agents based on the dichotomies described in the MBTI theory. For each attribute, it was sought to consider factors more consistent with a scenario of Sellers and Buyers distributed in the scenario (explained in more detail in the subsequent section). In this situation, each distinct agent will process the data perceived in the environment, and the information processing, conditioned to personality type, will influence its behavior.

3.2   The Seller-Buyer Model

Several researchers have already used the approach with entities defined as Sellers, and Buyers [7, 29, 32] to observe situations closer to the daily life seen in many organizations. In this model, two types of agents are defined, Buyers and Sellers, having distinct particularities and generally interacting over a pre-defined time interval. The possibilities of actions derived from these interactions are many, but in this work, we will use the same approach already demonstrated in [3].

Buyers. Buyers represent companies, and they are distributed in fixed locations (they do not move). Their role is to wait for a Sellers' visit so they can perform a purchase transaction. They can only make purchases when their demand is greater than zero, and with each transaction, their purchase demand is reduced.

Sellers. Sellers have personalities conceived through the MBTI theory, and these decisively influence how they behave and decide. Initially, they wander the environment looking incessantly to visit Buyers and consequently make a sale. A priori, every visit from a Seller to a Buyer generates a sale transaction and subsequent purchase by the Buyer. Sellers also have a demand to sell, and as new transactions are made, their demand is also reduced. When it reaches the stipulated initial demand, the Seller is automatically removed from the environment.

3.3   Agent Decision Attributes

Following the architecture of the BDI and its subsequent extension to include the personalities types [21] adaptations have been made to the model [3] so that the Sellers agents could better assess their perceived inputs from the environment. In this way, five main attributes are used in the Sellers decision-making process:

Distance to the Buyer (A1) This attribute represents the Euclidean distance between a Seller and a Buyer and is considered as a cost attribute in MADM. As Sellers have a limited view of their environment, they cannot perceive all existing Buyers. This threshold also influences all other attributes.

Exploration or Exploitation (A2) The A2 attribute mainly impact the E-I dichotomy and was adapted from what was originally used in a previous study [3]. To better represent the influence of the Extraversion-Introversion dichotomy, we will represent here two types of attitudes: Exploration and Exploitation. Extraverted Sellers are more prone to Exploration. They tend to seek to meet Buyers they have never visited before. On the other hand, Introverts Sellers will seek the opposite, that is, to interact with Buyers they already know. This adaptation seems to be more coherent with the notions of inner and outer world described in MBTI [16–18]. To measure the attribute, we will use the number of visits made by the Seller to the respective Buyers; For extraverted agents it will be counted as a benefit attribute in MADM. At the same time, it will be a cost attribute for introverts.

Cluster Density and Proximity to the Perception Edge (A3) For this attribute, adaptations were also made to include characteristics closer to the S-N dichotomy. With this attribute, Sellers can perceive the density of the Buyers cluster, thus making it possible to abstract future gains. In this attribute, the proximity of Buyers to the edge of the Sellers' perception radius will also be considered, so more imaginative Sellers can think that other Buyers may be close to the limit of their perception radius, envisioning future gains. We calculate both as benefit attributes in MADM, however, Intuition Sellers will prioritize cluster density and proximity to the edge of perception, while Sensing Sellers will prioritize the distance to the Buyer.

Sellers Close to the Target-Buyer (A4) The T-F dichotomy has the main influence on this attribute, considered as a cost attribute in MADM. In this attribute, Sellers will consider whether there are other co-workers close to the same objective (Buyer) who they have. Feeling Sellers prioritize what other Sellers can aim for, seeking out Buyers who are not close to their colleagues. Thinking Sellers tend to be rational and more concerned with the goals defined by the organization.

Probability to Recalculate the Plan (A5) This attribute is influenced by the J-P dichotomy and is directly implemented in agents as a probability of reconsidering their decisions. The attribute deals with how committed the Seller is to maintaining its original plan. Perceiving Sellers will constantly reconsider their decisions based on changing environment conditions. However, Judging Sellers will tend to keep to their original plan even if other alternatives appear along the way to the chosen Buyer.

3.4   Market Types

To evaluate the agents' performance, different scenarios were defined inspired by the Law of Supply and Demand [12]. For reasons of simplicity, we will not use the price variable; that is, in the experiments that will be demonstrated, all agents do not suffer the impact that an eventual price variation could cause in the market. Thus, we will analyze how the influence of demand variation may or may not impact the performance of Sellers agents, decreasing or not their delivery capacity. For this, three different market types were defined:

Balanced Market In this scenario, both agents, Sellers, and Buyers, have similar buying and selling demands, that is, the market has a general balance of demand.

Supply Market In this market, Sellers have a higher sales demand than the Buyers' purchase demand. This is a more challenging scenario for Sellers as there is a restriction on Buyers' purchasing potential.

Demand Market Finally, there may be a market in which the purchase demand is greater than the Sellers are able or need to meet, thus existing an imbalance in which the Buyers will not have their demand fully met.

3.5   Work Teams

Another essential aspect implemented in the current model is the notion of work teams. Previous studies noticed a focus on agents individually, analyzing the relationship between their performance and personality type. With the concept of work teams, we will seek to analyze how the composition of different agent teams with different personality type profiles can influence the groups' overall performance. Work teams are defined as interdependent collections of individuals who share responsibility for specific outcomes for their organizations [26]. Individuals in a team usually have one or more common goals and jointly seek to achieve these goals by performing tasks relevant to an organizational context [14,15]. So, in this work, we will analyze the influence of the behavioral preference in teams of Sellers agents, observing the impact of the different personality type profiles on the performance of the teams.

3.6   Hypotheses

Given the challenges already discussed about forming high-performance teams, a first research question emerges: Can Seller agent teams modeled with different personality types present different performance levels? To advance this study, we will seek to analyze how teams of agents formed with opposite behaviors perform. For simplicity, we will focus on the Extraversion-Introversion dichotomy in which future studies may expand the scope to other dichotomies. This leads us to formulate the first hypothesis of the study.

Hypothesis 1 (H1): *There is a performance difference between Teams composed of extraverted and introverted agents.*

With this hypothesis, we seek to analyze whether the two opposing behavioral preferences, extraversion and introversion, can lead Sellers' teams to have different performances given the common attitude of the group of agents. To be able to analyze if other factors associated with the environment could influence the performance of agent teams, we also formulated a second hypothesis:

Hypothesis 2 (H2): *Markets with different Supply and Demand levels can impact the teams' performance.*

In this case, we seek to analyze whether agent teams with different personality type profiles can be impacted, for example, by types of market in which there are demand restrictions, both for sale and purchase.

4 Methods and Results

The experiments were performed using a model developed and implemented in the Gama platform, making use of the architecture *simple_bdi* [28]. The platform allows a high-level language to build agent-based models, making it possible to observe behaviors and interactions between agents with different levels of abstraction [8]. Perception functions were also used to enable Sellers to perceive Buyers and also other Sellers around them. We defined a perception radius that limits the number of agents that they can perceive; thus, Sellers have a restricted view of what they can see around them. However, as they walk through the environment, they can visualize agents that they did not know before, thus expanding their knowledge of the environment.

Both Sellers and Buyers have initial locations defined through random seed, so we can use the same initial conditions for each simulation performed, changing only the different personalities type of the work teams we want to evaluate. We also used pre-defined cycles for each simulation, causing agents to have a time limit to complete their tasks. At the end of the simulations, we evaluate the Sellers' teams' performance, measuring the number of products sold to the respective Buyers.

4.1 Environment Setup

We used a Grid size of 125×125 with a maximum of 250 cycles for each simulation to carry out the experiments. We also set the rates for the number of

Buyers and Sellers respectively as 2.0% and 0.5%, thus totaling 313 Buyers and 78 Sellers. This choice was made to maintain an approximately four times higher ratio of Buyers to Sellers, representing a scenario with a low density of Buyers.

The total number of products to be sold by the Sellers and purchased by the Buyers was fixed and defined as 4.688 products. As Sellers can choose to revisit a Buyer, we define as three the maximum number of visits that a Seller can make to the same Buyer. We also added a parameter that defines the number of cycles a Seller needs to wait until they can revisit a Buyer, set this to 75 (30% of the total number of cycles). These initial parameters were empirically defined through observations carried out in several simulations. With the observations made it was possible to analyze, for example, how long it would take for 80% of Buyers to have at least one visit at the end of each simulation.

In further works, it is intended to explore other scenario configurations and variations of the initial parameters (such as the number of agents, grid size, agents' perception radius, initial agent's demand, among others), thus providing more robust analyzes considering other situations not addressed in the current work.

To handle the distribution of the products in the different market types, we defined a product division strategy following each market type. For the Balanced Market, the 4.688 products were divided into 2.344 products to be sold and other 2.344 to be purchased. In each group of Buyers and Sellers these values were equally divided among the agents. In the Supply Market, we divided 2/3 of the products to the Sellers and 1/3 to the Buyers, corresponding respectively to 3.120 sale products, and the Buyers with a demand of 1.565 products. The same numbers were applied in the Demand Market, switching these values: 2/3 of the products to the Buyers and 1/3 to the Sellers.

4.2 Experiments

To evolve with the formulated hypotheses, we used different compositions of work team profiles, combining certain behavioral preferences with other random combinations, thus allowing us to analyze the influence of each agent teams'

Table 1. Team profiles

Profile	Attitude	Personality type	Profile	Attitude	Personality type
PROF1	Extraverted	E+random	PROF8	Introverted	I+random
PROF2	Extraverted	ES+random	PROF9	Introverted	IS+random
PROF3	Extraverted	EN+random	PROF10	Introverted	IN+random
PROF4	Extraverted	EST+random	PROF11	Introverted	IST+random
PROF5	Extraverted	ESF+random	PROF12	Introverted	ISF+random
PROF6	Extraverted	ENT+random	PROF13	Introverted	INT+random
PROF7	Extraverted	ENF+random	PROF14	Introverted	INF+random

personality type. Table 1 shows these different team profiles. In addition to these fourteen teams, we will also consider a completely random profile (PROF15) aiming to also have heterogeneous team compositions.

For each scenario, we ran 15 simulations, each of them composed of a given team profile. In these experiments, we used a same random seed for all team profiles, thus ensuring the same initial conditions for all simulations. Moreover, to mitigate the fact that a given random seed could benefit a specific profile, we performed these 15 simulations with 5 different random seed values, resulting in a total number of 75 simulations for each scenario. Thus, we obtained a sample larger than 30 observations to ensure greater significance in the statistical test. The obtained results for the Balanced, Supply and Demand Markets are shown respectively in Figures in Fig. 1(a), Fig. 1(b) and Fig. 1(c).

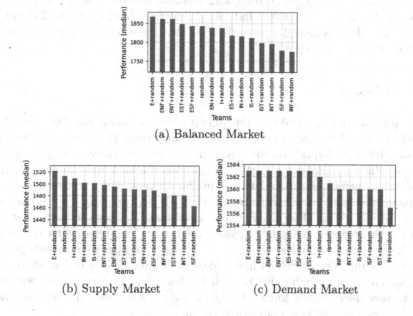

(a) Balanced Market

(b) Supply Market   (c) Demand Market

Fig. 1. Team profile performance in different scenarios

4.3   Obtained Results

In order to analyze the performance results of the experiments carried out, we applied the Wilcoxon [30] test to compare team profiles with an extraverted or introverted tendency and thus be able to answer the first hypothesis *(H1)* for each market. For this end, we have added the results obtained by PROF1–PROF7, typically extroverted, with the ones obtained by PROF8–PROF14, that correspond to the introverted type. The completely random profile PROF15 was not considered in this test.

For the Balanced Market, we obtained *p-value* = 0.000023, indicating that we can reject the *Null Hypothesis (H0)* and thus conclude that there is a difference between the extraverted and introverted profiles. For the Supply Market, we obtained *p-value* = 0.229537, indicating that in this case, we cannot reject *H0*, and thus we conclude that there are no differences between the profiles. For the Demand Market, the *p-value* = 0.000272 allows us to conclude that there are also differences between the profiles. Despite of these results, as we will see in Sect. 5, the difference does not seem significant when analyzing the percentage of demand reached by each agent team.

We also analyze the second hypothesis *(H2)* using the Wilcoxon test, comparing the performance of each of the fifteen team profiles in the three different scenarios, on a two by two basis. That is, we compare the same profiles in the scenarios: Balanced Market with Supply Market, Balanced Market with Demand Market and Supply Market with Demand Market. For all comparisons, we obtained *p-value* = 0.000002, indicating that we can reject the *Null Hypothesis (H0)*, i.e., there is indeed a performance difference when we analyze the same profile in different scenarios.

5   Discussion

Based on simulations carried out, the highest performances in the Balanced Market were obtained by Extravert agent teams, indicating that their Exploratory attitude with a predisposition to expand their sales area allowed them to obtain better results than Introverts agent teams. Because they are more shy, introverted Seller agents tend to relate to familiar Buyers, which makes it difficult to expand their sales area and consequently their performance. The second and third positions obtained by agent teams ENF and ENT also indicate that the intuitive characteristic with the tendency to abstract long-term gains, combined with the exploration profile, brought the teams a competitive advantage. We also see that Introverted Sellers had a lower performance in a Balanced Market scenario. This was probably due to their tendency to seek interactions with the same Buyers they already know. As they are more shy, they tend to keep their usual Buyers avoiding new unexplored regions.

In a more challenging market where Supply is higher than Demand, there is no difference between the Extraverted and Introverted agent teams. This result can be explained because, in a scarcer market, where Buyers quickly do not have more additional demand, Introverted Sellers should have an exploratory attitude in order to adapt to the given conditions, seeking new opportunities and consequently have greater performances. As seen earlier, this change can suggest a better adaptation of the agent teams to the environment, and although not the purpose of this study, it is in line with the understanding of the MBTI theory on the development of skills and talents [18].

When the scenario is changed to a market where Demand is higher than Supply, the results indicated that there are differences between the performances of Extraverted and Introverted Seller agents teams. Despite this, it is important to note that all teams achieved over 99% of their initial demands; we can consider that all teams had excellence in their performance and the personality type was not a relevant factor in this type of market. It was also clear from the experiments that the type of market can decisively influence the performance of the Sellers agents, limiting their ability to act and influencing their results.

It is essential to explain that the purpose of this model is not to assess whether certain types of personalities are better or worse for performing the tasks [3], which would even represent a misuse of the MBTI [6]. The analyses and interpretations carried out from this study should be restricted to the scope of the model shown, which is not a tool for selecting or stereotyping individuals. The study is also limited to the analysis of artificial agent teams, and these do not represent reality; that is, although the study can support a greater understanding of characteristics associated with the personality types described in the MBTI, these should not be directly associated with people's life. The interpretations must be restricted to the scope of experiments based on agents considered in this work.

In further work, new metrics that allow the analysis of exploration and exploitation attitudes may also contribute to a greater guarantee of assertiveness in the conclusions about the results. Price variations in the markets and negotiation mechanisms between Sellers and Buyers agents could also be implemented, thus making it possible to observe more complex situations and close to those observed in organizational environments. Other approaches explored by studies such as [9, 10] can also be integrated to complement aspects related to the team composition as well as helping to a better understanding of factors that might be related to agents' performance.

References

1. Alvares, L.O., Sichman, J.S.: Introduçao aos sistemas multiagentes. In: XVII Congresso da SBC-Anais JAI 1997 (1997)
2. Bratman, M.E., Israel, D.J., Pollack, M.E.: Plans and resource-bounded practical reasoning. Comput. Intell. **4**(3), 349–355 (1988)
3. Braz, L.F., Sichman, J.S.: Using MBTI agents to simulate human behavior in a work context. In: Czupryna, M., Kamiński, B. (eds.) Advances in Social Simulation. SPC, pp. 329–341. Springer, Cham (2022). https://doi.org/10.1007/978-3-030-92843-8_25
4. Braz, L.F., Sichman, J.S.: Using the Myers-Briggs Type Indicator (MBTI) for modeling multiagent systems. Revista de Informática Teórica e Aplicada **29**(1), 42–53 (2022)
5. Braz, L.F., Sichman, J.S.: Um estudo do myers-briggs type indicator (mbti) para modelagem de sistemas multiagentes no apoio a processos de recrutamento e seleção nas empresas. In: Anais do XIV Workshop-Escola de SistemasAgentes, seus Ambientes e apliCações de Agentes, seus Ambientes e apliCações, pp. 250–255. Zenodo (2020)
6. Coe, C.K.: The MBTI: potential uses and misuses in personnel administration. Public Pers. Manag. **21**(4), 511–522 (1992)

7. DeLoach, S.A.: Modeling organizational rules in the multi-agent systems engineering methodology. In: Cohen, R., Spencer, B. (eds.) AI 2002. LNCS (LNAI), vol. 2338, pp. 1–15. Springer, Heidelberg (2002). https://doi.org/10.1007/3-540-47922-8_1

8. Drogoul, A., et al.: GAMA: a spatially explicit, multi-level, agent-based modeling and simulation platform. In: Demazeau, Y., Ishida, T., Corchado, J.M., Bajo, J. (eds.) PAAMS 2013. LNCS (LNAI), vol. 7879, pp. 271–274. Springer, Heidelberg (2013). https://doi.org/10.1007/978-3-642-38073-0_25

9. Farhangian, M.: Capturing the effect of personality on teams with agent-based modelling. Ph.D. thesis, University of Otago (2018)

10. Farhangian, M., Purvis, M., Purvis, M., Savarimuthu, B.T.R.: Modelling the effects of personality and temperament in the team formation process. In: the First International Workshop on Multiagent Foundations of Social Computing, at The 13th International Joint Conference on Autonomous Agents & Multiagent Systems, Paris, vol. 6 (2014)

11. Furnham, A., Stringfield, P.: Personality and work performance: Myers-Briggs Type Indicator correlates of managerial performance in two cultures. Personality Individ. Differ. 14(1), 145–153 (1993)

12. Heakal, R.: Economics basics: Supply and demand. Investopedia. Accessed 28 Sep 2015

13. Jung, C.G.: Obras Completas de C. G. Jung, Editora Vozes Limitada (2011)

14. Kozlowski, S.W., Ilgen, D.R.: Enhancing the effectiveness of work groups and teams. Psychol. Sci. Public Interest 7(3), 77–124 (2006)

15. Mathieu, J.E., Hollenbeck, J.R., van Knippenberg, D., Ilgen, D.R.: A century of work teams in the journal of applied psychology. J. Appl. Psychol. 102(3), 452 (2017)

16. Myers, I.B.: Introduction to type: a guide to understanding your results on the Myers-Briggs Type Indicator. Mountain View, CA: CPP (1998)

17. Myers, I.B., McCaulley, M.H., Quenk, N.L., Hammer, A.L.: MBTI Manual: A Guide to the Development and Use of the Myers-Briggs Type Indicator, vol. 3. Consulting Psychologists Press Palo Alto, CA (1998)

18. Myers, I.B., Myers, P.B.: Gifts Differing: Understanding Personality Type. Nicholas Brealey, Boston (2010)

19. Padgham, L., Lambrix, P.: Agent capabilities: extending BDI theory. In: AAAI/IAAI, pp. 68–73 (2000)

20. Rao, A.S., Georgeff, M.P., et al.: BDI agents: from theory to practice. In: Icmas, vol. 95, pp. 312–319 (1995)

21. Salvit, J.: Extending BDI with Agent Personality Type. Ph.D. thesis, The City University of New York (2012)

22. Salvit, J., Sklar, E.: Toward a Myers-Briggs Type Indicator model of agent behavior in multiagent teams. In: Bosse, T., Geller, A., Jonker, C.M. (eds.) MABS 2010. LNCS (LNAI), vol. 6532, pp. 28–43. Springer, Heidelberg (2011). https://doi.org/10.1007/978-3-642-18345-4_3

23. Salvit, J., Sklar, E.: Modulating agent behavior using human personality type. In: Proceedings of the Workshop on Human-Agent Interaction Design and Models (HAIDM) at Autonomous Agents and MultiAgent Systems (AAMAS), pp. 145–160 (2012)

24. Sharp, J.M., Hides, M., Bamber, C.J., Castka, P.: Continuous Organisational learning through the development of high performance teams. In: ICSTM (2000)

25. Stanujkic, D., Magdalinovic, N., Jovanovic, R.: A multi-attribute decision making model based on distance from decision maker's preferences. Informatica **24**(1), 103–118 (2013)
26. Sundstrom, E., De Meuse, K.P., Futrell, D.: Work teams: applications and effectiveness. Am. Psychol. **45**(2), 120 (1990)
27. Sycara, K.P.: Multiagent systems. AI Magazine **19**(2), 79 (1998)
28. Taillandier, P., Bourgais, M., Caillou, P., Adam, C., Gaudou, B.: A BDI agent architecture for the GAMA modeling and simulation platform. In: Nardin, L.G., Antunes, L. (eds.) MABS 2016. LNCS (LNAI), vol. 10399, pp. 3–23. Springer, Cham (2017). https://doi.org/10.1007/978-3-319-67477-3_1
29. Tran, T., Cohen, R.: A learning algorithm for buying and selling agents in electronic marketplaces. In: Cohen, R., Spencer, B. (eds.) AI 2002. LNCS (LNAI), vol. 2338, pp. 31–43. Springer, Heidelberg (2002). https://doi.org/10.1007/3-540-47922-8_3
30. Wilcoxon, F.: Individual comparisons by ranking methods. In: Kotz, S., Johnson, N.L. (eds.) Breakthroughs in Statistics. Springer Series in Statistics, pp. 196–202. Springer, New York (1992). https://doi.org/10.1007/978-1-4612-4380-9_16
31. Williams, K.: Developing High Performance Teams. Elsevier, Amsterdam (2004)
32. Xu, H., Shatz, S.M.: An agent-based petri net model with application to seller/buyer design in electronic commerce. In: Proceedings 5th International Symposium on Autonomous Decentralized Systems, pp. 11–18. IEEE (2001)

Reconsidering an Agent-Based Model of Food Web Evolution

Samuel Armstrong and Emma Norling[(✉)] [iD]

Department of Computer Science, The University of Sheffield, Sheffield, UK
e.j.norling@sheffield.ac.uk

Abstract. This paper reimplements and extends a prior agent-based model of food web evolution. The earlier work attempted to replicate the results achieved by a system dynamics model of food web evolution, but failed to achieve the diversity or realistic dynamics of the system dynamics approach. This work starts by adding spatial diversity to the model, the lack of this being flagged as a potential problem in the original work. This produced some improvement in the results (with more diverse food webs being produced), but there were still patterns commonly found in the resultant food webs that are uncommon in real-world food webs. To further refine the model, a more complex representation of species traits was added, and methods for classifying species based upon the traits. In particular, an unsupervised learning clustering algorithm has been introduced to classify species in the evolving food web. This has resulted in a model which produces abstract food webs that far more closely mimic the patterns found in real-world food webs.

Keywords: Agent-Based simulation · Spatial representation · Food webs

1 Introduction

The way in which a food web evolves to support diversity in an ecosystem has long been a key area of interest for ecological scientists. One method for unlocking some of the complex dynamics behind the evolution of a food web is by simulating it artificially. This has been attempted many times, using many different methodologies and strategies, all with varying degrees of success. The work described in this paper builds upon earlier work by Norling [10], which attempted to create an agent-based model of food web dynamics that mirrored a more traditional system dynamics model. That work did demonstrate the emergence of some simple food webs, but "complex food webs do not arise, even for runs over extended periods." A number of possible reasons were postulated in the original paper, particularly the lack of a spatial representation, which meant there were few advantages to the specialisation of species. Despite these issues, the agent-based model showed "a certain level of correspondence to the system dynamics model," and the paper also acknowledged that an "agent-based model

© The Author(s), under exclusive license to Springer Nature Switzerland AG 2023
F. Lorig and E. Norling (Eds.): MABS 2022, LNAI 13743, pp. 70–81, 2023.
https://doi.org/10.1007/978-3-031-22947-3_6

will allow the exploration of a range of variations that would be difficult (if not impossible) to encode in the system dynamics model."

In this project, the original work was replicated, using a modern framework (as agent-based modelling frameworks have evolved considerably in the intervening period), and subsequent iterations looked at the effect of considering spatial diversity and heterogenous behaviour of the agents. The results of these extensions demonstrate a far higher ability to parallel the diversity of species and relationships between species that are observed in real world food webs. Section 2 looks at food webs and their evolution, as well as considering the challenges of modelling these types of systems. Section 3 explains the (reimplementation of) the original model by Norling, and Sect. 4 considers first the addition of a notion of spatial diversity, and second, the addition of heterogeneous behaviour (dependent on agent characteristics) which evolves with species. The paper concludes in Sect. 5 with a summary and ideas for future work.

2 Food Webs and Their Evolution

In simple terms, food webs are a network of all the predator-prey relationships that exist in a particular ecosystem, and these evolve along with the species within them. According to the Darwinian theory of evolution by natural selection, species will evolve based on a natural bias towards traits that offer them an advantage to survival within their ecosystem [6]. There are a wide variety of traits that are desirable for species in each ecosystem that relate to all aspects of survival. For example, it may benefit a species to have excellent eyesight as this will help them hunt for prey – allowing them to survive; but equally it may benefit them to have thick fur to help them maintain body heat in a cold environment. Each of these factors benefits the survival of the species, though they help the species in very different ways.

As alluded to by Brown, Reilly and Peet [2], there are many external factors that affect which traits are beneficial for a particular species. These include geographic factors, such as different physical features occurring in the environment; biological features, such as competition; and environmental features, such as the availability of resources. Combinations of these factors create a wide array of opportunities in the environment for species to evolve and fill their own niche spot in the food web. This may be especially true with geographical features, as certain characteristics will heavily favour a species if it lives in one environment, but may not be an advantage at all if it lives in another environment. For example, a species could evolve to be very small to easily hide in the cracks of a rock formation where it lives, but if it was living in the nearby desert, its size would not help it hide and would mean that it was prey to a lot of other species.

It is the combination of all the factors above that, over millions of years of evolution, leads to the vast speciation and diversity seen in food webs.

2.1   Patterns Observed in Real-World Food Webs

There are a few characteristic patterns that are often observed in real-world food webs. One such characteristic is the presence of trophic levels. Trophic levels in an ecosystem are groups of species that represent one stage of the transfer of energy up the food chain. As an example, both sharks and orca don't have any natural predators, meaning they are on the highest level of the food web, usually level four or five. Food webs are usually large and complex, depending on the biodiversity of a given ecosystem, and are constantly changed according to the evolution and extinction of species [9]. Food webs also tend to have a feed-forward structure where species in the higher trophic levels feed on species in the lower trophic levels. This is a almost universal principle, with there being few instances where a lower trophic level species can feed on a higher trophic level species, and even the presence of bi-directional connections – where two species can feed on each other – is generally a very rare phenomena. Another characteristic is that omnivores rarely occur as food webs containing them "tend to be less stable than webs without omnivory" [8]. These are the sort of characteristics that would ideally be observed in a simulation of the evolution of a food web.

2.2   Population Dynamics

Various studies reinforce the need to understand the changing size and structure of a population over time (recent examples include [1,5,7]). The population dynamics are the underlying cause of the system-level effects seen in populations – so in order to accurately depict the diversity found in real-world food webs, it is important to accurately simulate the population dynamics that ultimately lead to this diversity. Traditional methods of simulation often use mathematical models, or a 'system dynamics' approach [10], to attempt to recreate some of these dynamics. These models can, however, over-simplify the population dynamics, which can lead to simulations that do not act in the same manner as real-world food webs. As an example, Rossberg [12] explains that models like this may use an ordinary differential equation to model the exponential growth of a population. However, they do not take into account additional factors, such as the effect of the exponentially growing species on the environment they live in, which would make the real-life effect differ from the simulated effect.

Morin and Lawler [8] identify some of the key population dynamics that have been observed in real-world food webs. The first of these is that food webs of greater complexity tend to have a less stable structure, thus potentially leading to more instances of species extinction or changes in the species that are thriving. Similarly, the introduction or mutation of new species in the environment can have significant impact on the existing population, such as over-predating species or making species uncompetitive, which would likely lead to the extinction of those species. This is one of the key principles of the evolution of food webs, and can be observed in the real world. For example, the introduction of cane toads in Australia has caused a large reduction in the population size of many of the predator species that already existed in the environment, as the toads were better adapted to survival than other species, making the existing species uncompetitive [3]. In addition, if a new species appeared that could take advantage of a niche spot in the environment, such as an inhospitable location, then further species may be able to evolve to feed on this new species.

Overall, population dynamics mean that real-world food webs are an ever-changing network of species that are constantly evolving. When observed over significant time periods, food webs are never completely stable. These are all types of dynamics that should be sought after for a successful simulation of the temporal evolution of food webs.

3   Reimplementation of the Previous Agent-Based Model

Rather than try to work with code that was written for a very old version of Repast Simphony [11], the key features of that model (as described in [10]) were reimplemented using NetLogo [14]. This was largely a pragmatic step, as NetLogo has a less steep learning curve than Repast. Figure 1 shows an example of the interface for this reimplementation.

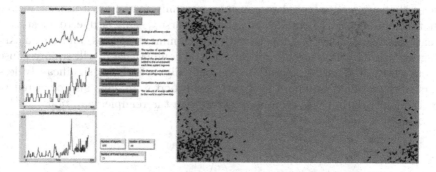

Fig. 1. A snapshot showing a run of the reimplemented model in NetLogo. The graphs display (from top to bottom) the number of agents in the model, the number of species in the model, and the number of food web connections in the model as a function of time. On the right-hand side, different colours represent different species of agents.

In the description of the original model, it was not clear whether agents should be able to consume agents of their own species. In the reimplementation, experiments were done with this both turned on and off, keeping all other factors consistent. It was found that if agents were not allowed to consume agents of their own species, this would lead to one extremely dominant species that destroys any diversity in the ecosystem. In contrast, when they were allowed to consume their own species, it meant that there was a more diverse array of species that were able to co-exist in the environment. Therefore, the decision was made to allow agents to consume their own species for this reimplementation. This essentially means each individual agent is only trying to survive itself and does not consider the health its species as a whole, which is a trait that can be observed in many animal species alive today.

The aim of the original work was to replicate the results from a system dynamics model of food web evolution [4], and as in that system dynamics model, the species within the model do not correspond to those in any particular natural ecosystem, but are stylised species, each defined by a set of features. The features themselves are also abstract - conceptually they could be things such as "tough skin", "fast locomotion" or such; things that could potentially give them an edge over other species. In this reimplementation the same principles have been followed.

3.1 Results from This Model

The food webs produced by the reimplemented model, such as Fig. 2, consistently find that species which solely rely on predation struggle to survive, whereas species that consume both other agents and the world have a much better rate of survival. This leads to food webs that have a somewhat unrealistic structure, as species are well adapted to feed on everything, whereas in real-world food webs, species generally adapt to feed on specific food sources. In addition, having species that are well adapted to consume anything in the environment means that the food web lacks significant species diversity. This is due to most new species not being able to compete with the dominant species, and so quickly dying out, and when a species appears that is competitive it will simply cause the currently dominating species to die out. Figure 2 shows significantly less diversity than would be found in a real-world food web. This also occurred in the original work, but was even more extreme in the reimplementation.

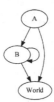

Fig. 2. A typical food web produced by the reimplemented model.

One of the issues with food webs as shown in Fig. 2 is that the higher-level species (A) has a strong advantage over the lower-level one (B): they can feed *both* from the environment and from the other species. This leads to an explosion in the population of A, followed by the extinction of population B, and then a return to lower levels of population A (due to the decrease in food sources). This contrasts with a more classical balance of species that is often considered in agent-based modelling, such as wolf and sheep [13] or foxes and rabbits. In such models, one sees a growth in the predator species as they feast upon their prey, but as the prey becomes scarce, so too do predator numbers fall, due to lack of food.

This reimplemented model generally produces very similar results to those found with the original model, both in terms of the dynamics observed and the food webs produced. As an example, the lack of pure predators found in the food web was also an issue in the original model, and it meant that only simple food webs could be produced. Having this problem appearing in the models shows a good level of correspondence of the reimplemented to the original model, but is an issue that certainly needs to be addressed in future models. The inclusion of a spatial representation in this model did not seem to have any significant impact on the results when compared to the original model. This was somewhat expected, as the literature survey identified a spatial representation as being a tool to unlock new possibilities for improving the agent-based model, but not necessarily being a major improvement on its own. In addition, the use of random rather than fixed mutation did n0t seem to have a significant impact, which was beneficial as the inclusion of the parameter was only due to ambiguity in the original work.

As can be seen in Table 1, the model only sustains an average of 1.623 species. This quantitatively backs up the observation of the lack of food web diversity produced by this model and provides a point of comparison for comparing the diversity of the food webs of this model to other models produced in this project.

4   Enhancements to the Model

Replication of the baseline model confirmed the shortcomings observed in [10]; the real aim of this work was to try to improve upon those results. The first step towards this was to introduce a constant decay rate of the energy level of agents. This means that the energy level for each agent is reduced by a constant amount in each time step, resulting in an agent's death if their energy falls to zero. In addition, a different approach to distributing energy from the world to the agents is introduced: a plant species which can be consumed by agents with appropriate characteristics (that is, characteristics determine how successfully the agents can gain energy from plants). The plants are then being removed from that place in the environment for a refractory period whilst they 'regrow'.

4.1   Geographic "niches"

Distinct geographic regions are introduced to the environment, creating additional niche spots in the environment that species can adapt to fill, which is one of the key factors in the speciation of real-world animals. Thus, this change should support a greater diversity of species that are able to survive in the environment. The different environments will be modelled as containing different species of plants, so as to have differentiation between the different areas (and different animals will 'prefer' – that is, consume energy more successfully from

– different plants). To put into context how these species of plants define geographic regions, an example in nature is cacti being in the desert and tall trees existing in the rainforest. Animals have to adapt to consume these in the same way that agents would need to adapt to consume different plants in the model.

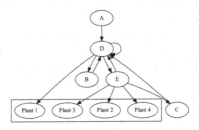

Fig. 3. A typical food web produced in a model with geographic specialisation.

Figure 3 shows the food web created from one run of the extended model, after around 3000 time steps. The initial observation upon viewing this food web is the additional complexity it contains compared to any food web found with the reimplemented model, sustaining five species on top of the four plant species. This immediately addresses one of the primary issues with the reimplemented model – the lack of diversity found in the food webs produced by the model. In addition, the roles that species are playing in this food web are much better defined and are more comparable to real-world food webs, with one clear basal species and an apex predator. The food web produced is split into four distinct trophic levels, starting with the plants as the first level. Species E is the primary basal species, which is capable of feeding upon most of the plants in the environment. The energy then propagates up the food web to the next trophic level, containing species D. Species D is the sole predator of species E, although it is actually an omnivorous species as it can also consume plant 1. Species A, B and C are all predators that have no capability to eat plants, so solely rely on predation to survive. These form the final trophic level of the food web, with species A being the apex predator as it has no predators.

There are some patterns in this food web that do not correspond to what might be expected in a real-world food web. For example, Fig. 3 shows a 'cycle' of connections where species D can eat E, E can eat C, and C can eat D. Structures like this are highly uncommon in real world food webs. Energy is lost in the transfer from one trophic level to the next, which means that a cycle in a food web should not be able to sustain itself. Another problem with the structure of the food webs produced is the presence of bi-directional connections, two of which can be seen in Fig. 3. While these occasionally do exist in real-world food webs, the frequency with which they occur in this model is unrealistic, once again to the nature of energy transfer between trophic levels.

By including the geographical areas in this model, the additional niche spots mean that this model overcomes the 'competitive exclusion principle' population dynamic that was occurring in the reimplemented model. Instead, the niche spots favour the evolution and survival of new species by some of the same principles that cause diversity in real-world food webs, which were highlighted in the literature survey.

4.2 Adding Heterogeneous Behaviour

Heterogeneous behaviour is where each species has a set of unique characteristics that determine their behaviour and abilities, each of which has a value. These values are on a continuous scale and represent traits that affect multiple aspects of their behaviour, rather than just their interactions, as was the case with the previous models. For example, an agent might have the ability to run faster, but this could come at the cost of a higher metabolism. In this version of the model, each agent has four features which are capable of mutation: predatory ability, plant eating ability, defence, and speed. To ensure that these values do not simply grow unconstrained, a fifth characteristic, metabolism, has been added which derives from these:

$$Metabolism = PredatoryAbility + PlantEatingAbility + Defence + \frac{Speed}{5} \quad (1)$$

This metabolism characteristic provides a trade-off for having better values for other characteristics, and thus prevents the values of these characteristics growing exponentially for the whole population. In this calculation the speed is divided by five as it is initialised as a value that is on average five times bigger than any of the other values, which are all initialised within the same range. In addition to agents having characteristics, plants will also have a set of characteristics which don't evolve over time, but do define different 'species' of plant according to the area in which they preside.

As in the previous models, an agent can eat another agent or plant when they are in the same geographic location. Whether or not a given agent can feed on another agent is defined by the following interaction rules:

$$x = \begin{cases} Eat, & \text{if } PredatoryAbility \times random(0, 2) > Defence \\ Ignore, & \text{otherwise} \end{cases} \quad (2)$$

The random value is designed to add a level of stochasticity to interactions, which should aid the evolution process. In addition to these rules, in this model, an agent cannot eat another agent that is of the same species as itself, and an agent cannot eat another agent that has a higher predatory ability score than itself.

In this model species reproduce in the same way as they did in the first two models – they produce an offspring once they are above a critical energy threshold. When an offspring is created, each of the feature values of the parent are randomly modified by a small amount, meaning the offspring is slightly mutated. This mechanic replaces the mutation mechanic of the first two models and makes this process more organic, as the mutated agents are able to find a niche over time by mutating further rather than immediately either finding a niche or not finding one – and either thriving or going extinct as a result.

An additional modification in this version was that instead of each area having a distinct plant species, each area has unique plant defence and plant energy values. The purpose of this is to allow species to adapt to particular regions, for example to adapt to an area that has a higher plant defence, but also has less competition. Watkins et al. (2015) used a similar method for differentiating between different geographic regions with great success. However, evaluation of this model determined that this method of differentiating the different environments was not as effective as the methods used in the extended model, which is perhaps due to the regions not being expressed by enough unique characteristics. Future work in this area could experiment with alternative methods or characteristic to describe the different regions.

The most challenging task with this variation was how to identify species within the model. In the previous models, there are clear boundaries which mean each agent has a clearly-defined species. In this variant, each agent has a unique feature vector of values rather than a species. The initial approach to this problem assigned each agent an individual class for each of each of its features. These classes were determined by how the agent's value for a given feature compared to the maximum value that any existing agent had for that feature. This feature would then be assigned a value from one to four depending on how its value compared. This was run for all the features of each agent and the array of classes assigned to an agent would determine its species – this is referred to as *linear species classification*. As can be seen in Fig. 4 (left example), this approach produces a diverse food web, but in fact *too* diverse – indicating that the classification mechanism might be dividing the agents into too many species.

To address this issue, a form of unsupervised learning clustering algorithm was introduced to identify species. To the best of our knowledge, unsupervised learning has never been used in this context before, so represents a novel approach to species classification in models of food web evolution. Many options for algorithms were considered and experimented with, but ultimately the DBSCAN clustering algorithm was applied, as it both runs reasonably quickly and, most importantly, does not require a predetermined number of clusters. The flexibility to produce an undefined number of clusters was a key attribute required for the problem, as the number of species that exists at any given time is not known. The DBSCAN algorithm works by starting with a random initial data point and looking for any other data points that are within a defined distance, epsilon, of it. If it finds any data points, these are added to the cluster and the algorithm will be run again to try to find any more data points are within the scope of any point in the cluster. Once no more data points can be found, if the size of the cluster exceeds a given threshold, min_samples, then the cluster will be finalised and the algorithm will randomly select a data point that is not in a cluster to continue the process. If the threshold is not met the data points found will not be assigned to a cluster.

This feature of the simulation was implemented in Python using NetLogo's 'py' extension. It used Scikit-Learn's 'cluster' module (Pedregosa et al., 2011), which was passed the values for each parameter of each agent that were standardised with a zero mean and unit variance using Scikit-Learn's 'StandardScaler' class. The value of epsilon used was 0.5 and the min_samples value used was 5. Python then returned the labels found by the algorithm to NetLogo, where they are used for plotting the number of species, colouring the agents according to their species, and finding the food web connections between the species.

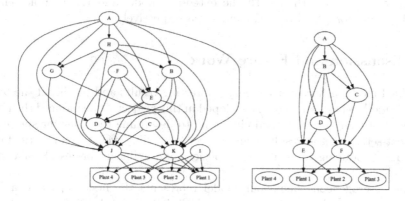

Fig. 4. Typical food webs produced in a model with heterogeneous behaviours. In the left-most example, species were identified using linear species classification, while in the right example, species were identified using unsupervised learning.

Figure 4 shows food webs that were created from typical runs of the simulation, with one using linear species classification on the left, and one using the unsupervised learning approach on the right. The first observable difference is their complexity. In the version with linear species classification (left), there are eleven species of agents in total, with a great deal of food web connections between the species. The food web also does not contain the bi-lateral connections or cycles that were found in the food webs of the extended model, meaning this food web has a more natural feedforward structure, with better defined trophic levels. There are around five trophic levels that can be seen in this food web, which lines up well with the number of trophic levels found in real-world food webs, per the literature survey. Likewise, this food web does not contain any omnivores, which the literature survey identified as a relatively rare occurrence, meaning this food web is certainly overall the most realistic that any model has produced during this project. This certainly shows initial promise to the model, but equally these results could be due to the linear species classification approach having too many possible categories for each characteristic.

Once again, with this unsupervised learning classification method the average number of species were considered, again over 500 steps, as shown in Table 1. The

Table 1. The average number of species evolved in runs of the different variants of the model (averaged over 500 time steps)

Run	1	2	3	4	5	Average
Replicated model	1.693	1.795	1.554	1.644	1.427	1.623
Geographic niches	5.691	7.365	4.397	4.084	5.093	5.326
Heterogenous behaviours	7.808	9.746	10.591	9.914	6.849	8.982

average number of species the is sustained in the heterogeneous behaviour model is significantly better than both the extended model and the reimplemented model – 8.982 compared to 5.326 and 1.623 respectively.

5   Discussion and Future Work

This final model achieved some very interesting results and produced the most realistic food webs of any model developed in this project. It introduced the novel approach of using unsupervised clustering to determine the different species in an agent-set, with the results achieved corresponding well to real world food-webs and producing more realistic species than a linear species classification approach.

The heterogeneous behaviour model represents the first steps into a new style of agent-based modelling of the evolution of food webs, showing that heterogeneous behaviour with unsupervised clustering is an interesting and fruitful concept for the purpose of simulating the evolution of a food web. Some such potential future improvements include:

- Multi-agent reproduction – currently all the models presented here have a simple system of reproduction, such that when any agent surpasses an energy threshold, an offspring agent is produced that has that same or slightly mutated characteristics from the parent. Including multi-agent reproduction (i.e. two agents to be together and offspring to have characteristics draw from both parents) would potentially help species adapt more effectively to local regions, as the individuals in that species would have to be in the same spatial location to reproduce.
- Additional wider environmental diversity – currently environmental niches are determined solely by the plant species that exist there. Varying terrain or water availability could allow more species to adapt to niche spots in the environment, leading to greater diversity of species.
- More descriptive features for agents – this could come in the form of adding additional features to agents, such as size or strength, or having the existing features more intricately describe agent behaviour (such as making the existing feature vector multi-dimensional with multiple vector values representing features like the predatory ability).

- Exploring further approaches for defining the species – such a different clustering algorithm or some form of tree structure that defines species based on the parents of agents.
- Increasing the model scale – including more environments and many more agents could help to yield more insightful results as these conditions better parallel those found in the real-world.

References

1. Bestley, S., et al.: Marine ecosystem assessment for the southern ocean: birds and marine mammals in a changing climate. Front. Ecol. Evol. **8**, 338 (2020)
2. Brown, R.L., Jacobs, L.A., Peet, R.K.: Species richness: small scale. eLS (2007)
3. Burnett, S.: Colonizing cane toads cause population declines in native predators: reliable anecdotal information and management implications. Pac. Conserv. Biol. **3**(1), 65–72 (1997)
4. Caldarelli, G., Higgs, P.G., McKane, A.J.: Modelling coevolution in multispecies communities. J. Theor. Biol. **193**(2), 345–358 (1998)
5. Campetella, G., et al.: Plant functional traits are correlated with species persistence in the herb layer of old-growth beech forests. Sci. Rep. **10**(1), 1–13 (2020)
6. Penguin Darwin, C., Bynum, W.F.: The origin of species by means of natural selection: or, the preservation of favored races in the struggle for life. Harmondsworth (2009)
7. Jouval, F., Bigot, L., Bureau, S., Quod, J.P., Penin, L., Adjeroud, M.: Diversity, structure and demography of coral assemblages on underwater lava flows of different ages at reunion island and implications for ecological succession hypotheses. Sci. Rep. **10**(1), 1–13 (2020)
8. Morin, P.J., Lawler, S.P.: Food web architecture and population dynamics: theory and empirical evidence. Annu. Rev. Ecol. Syst. **26**(1), 505–529 (1995)
9. National geographic society: food web. https://www.nationalgeographic.org/encyclopedia/food-web/. Accessed Jan 2022
10. Norling, E.: Contrasting a system dynamics model and an agent-based model of food web evolution. In: Antunes, L., Takadama, K. (eds.) MABS 2006. LNCS (LNAI), vol. 4442, pp. 57–68. Springer, Heidelberg (2007). https://doi.org/10.1007/978-3-540-76539-4_5
11. North, M.J., et al.: Complex adaptive systems modeling with Repast Simphony. Complex Adapt. Syst. Model. **1**(1), 1–26 (2013)
12. Rossberg, A.G.: Food Webs and Biodiversity: Foundations, Models, Data. John Wiley & Sons, Hoboken (2013)
13. Tatara, E., North, M., Howe, T., Collier, N., Vos, J., et al.: An indroduction to repast Simphony modeling using a simple predator-prey example. In: Proceedings of the Agent 2006 Conference on Social Agents: Results and Prospects. Citeseer (2006)
14. Tisue, S., Wilensky, U.: NetLogo: a simple environment for modeling complexity. In: International Conference on Complex Systems, vol. 21, pp. 16–21. Boston, MA (2004)

Surrogate Modeling of Agent-Based Airport Terminal Operations

Benyamin De Leeuw, S. Sahand Mohammadi Ziabari$^{(\boxtimes)}$ ⓘ,
and Alexei Sharpanskykh ⓘ

Delft University of Technology, Delft, The Netherlands
B.DeLeeuw@student.tudelft.nl, {S.S.mohamamdiziabari,
O.A.Sharpanskykh}@tudelft.nl

Abstract. The airport terminals are complex sociotechnical systems, which are difficult to understand and their behavior is hard to predict. Hence, an agent-based model, the Agent-based Airport Terminal Operation Model (AATOM), has been designed to represent and analyze diverse airport terminal processes, actors, their behavior and interactions. The main issue with such models is the large computational requirements for simulating detailed processes, making it computationally inefficient. Furthermore, the dynamics of such models are difficult to understand. Therefore, the goal of this research is to approximate the dynamics of AATOM by a surrogate model, while preserving the important system properties. A methodology is suggested for training and validating a surrogate model, based on the Random Forest algorithm. The trained surrogate model is capable of approximating the AATOM simulation and identifying relative importance of the model variables with respect to the model outputs. Firstly, the results obtained contain an evaluation of the surrogate model accuracy performance, indicating that the surrogate model can achieve an average accuracy of 93% in comparison to the original agent-based simulation model. Nonetheless, one indicator, the number of missed flights, has shown to be more difficult to predict, with an average accuracy of 83%. Secondly, the results show that the airport resource allocation has an important impact on the efficiency of the airport terminal, with the two most important variables being the number of desks at the check-in and the number of lanes at the checkpoint. Last, the developed surrogate model was compared with a second Artificial Neural Network-based surrogate model built for the same agent-based model.

Keywords: Surrogate modeling · Agent-based model · Random forest

1 Introduction

The airport terminal plays a crucial role in the modern air transportation system. Previous studies have focused on modelling and simulating the airport terminal operations, concentrating mainly on security analysis [1, 2]. For this purpose, An Agent-based Terminal Operation Model (AATOM) has been developed for modelling and analysis of complex sociotechnical airport systems with diverse interacting actors. The emergent

F. Lorig and E. Norling (Eds.): MABS 2022, LNAI 13743, pp. 82–94, 2023.
https://doi.org/10.1007/978-3-031-22947-3_7

in such complex systems is hard to understand [3]. Furthermore, AATOM has a high computational complexity. One of the approaches to improve understanding of agent-based models is surrogate modeling. In essence, it consists of generating a 'model of the model', obtaining an approximation of the original model. Surrogate modeling is used through various domains with the objective to emulate/surrogate an existing agent-based model [4]. Subsequently, the surrogate models are used for calibration [5], validation [6] or behavior space exploration [7].

Hence, two elements form the basis of the research, being the original AATOM model and surrogate modelling to abstract this model, to decrease its high computational complexity. Thus, the research objective is to obtain a computationally efficient AATOM while preserving the important dynamic (emergent) properties of the model and getting an insight into the underlying mechanisms of the model. The former underlines that by applying the surrogate modelling method (Random Forest) on the AATOM model, an approximation of the model can be obtained, preserving the system properties by accurately predicting the model output under given conditions. The latter is the ability of the approximation obtained from the original AATOM model to reveal the relations between the model inputs and outputs, leading to a better understanding of the system behavior. The main contributions of the study are the generation of a surrogate model from AATOM, the evaluation and validation of the surrogate model, and the comparison of the developed surrogate model (the Random Forest model) with another surrogate model (the ANN model) to gain better credibility in the obtained results.

In the following in this paper, background elements regarding AATOM and the surrogate model used for approximation are given in Sect. 2. Furthermore, the methodology developed for generating the surrogate model based on the AATOM is described in Sect. 3. Section 4 presents the results obtained by applying the methodology, focusing on the performance of the surrogate model and the input-output relationships. Last, the conclusions are drawn in Sect. 5.

2 Related Work

The AATOM is an agent-based simulation model used to represent the dynamics of passengers and airport terminal staff in the context of airport terminal operations [2, 26–28]. It comprises the agents with their properties, the environment and the interaction between the agents and the environment. The agent has a three-layered architecture, with each level adding a layer of abstraction. The three layers are: operational, tactical and strategical. In essence, the three-layered architecture dictates how the agent observes the environment and the other agents, and the way the agents interacts with both, based on the observations. Ultimately the agent is able to make decisions based on the beliefs about the environment and the other agents. For a more detailed description of the AATOM architecture we refer to [2]. The environment is composed of three objects: the areas, the flights and the physical objects. The first being two-dimensional polygons that delimit the different terminal areas (check-in, checkpoint, entrance, gate and facility).

Surrogate modeling is the approach for generating an approximation of the model in order to reduce its complexity while maintaining the dynamic properties of the original model. A surrogate model can be constructed by using a learning algorithm to obtain an abstraction of the model. This study considers two types of surrogate models. The first model is developed using the methodology described in Sect. 3. The second is used for comparison purposes and a brief explanation of its elaboration is given. The algorithm chosen for generating the first surrogate model, is the Random Forest. This learning algorithm has been proven to be a reliable and efficient method for working with large data-sets, achieving low computational costs [8]. In addition, the implementation of the algorithm for surrogate modelling is relatively simple [9–11]. Furthermore, there are classification and regression trees, differing on the nature of the target variable, being qualitative or quantitative respectively. In this research only regression trees are considered as the AATOM output target variables are only continuous. The target variables, represent different airport terminal indicators measuring processing times or counting the passenger flux. In addition, the Random Forest method has a specific measure for ranking the different parameters on their relative importance, called the variable importance measure (VIM) [12]. Measuring the relative importance of the variables can identify specific relations between the model variables and indicators. Giving additional insights into the underlying relationships of the original (AATOM) model [13]. The second model is based on Artificial Neural Network (ANN). The key motivation to use ANN is the low computational cost and the capability of approximation. ANNs have good generalization properties, can deal with large datasets and are able to represent nonlinearity. However, vanishing gradient is the main problem of ANN in the back propagation. In order to measure the sensitivity of parameters, different algorithms, mainly focusing on the connection weights in artificial neural networks, have been proposed. In [14] feature selection is described as 'the problem of choosing as small subset of features that ideally is necessary and sufficient to describe the target concept'. The main issue with the previous algorithm [15] was that when the training finished, it naturally assumed that the higher the amount of weights, the more important a parameter while regularization techniques make weights to not increase and become smaller [16]. The method which we used to measure the relative importance of parameters is called variance-based feature importance [17]. This is based on the principle that the more important is a parameter, the more the weights, which are connected to the corresponding input neurons, vary during the training of the model. To measure the relative importance of each parameter, variances of each weight connected to the input layer is calculated in the training time [18]. The algorithm that we used for computing these variances is an adaptation of Welford's online algorithm [17] for computing these variances.

3   Methodology

A step-wise systematic iterative procedure is defined in order to obtain an accurate approximation of AATOM by surrogate modelling. The schematic representation is given in Fig. 1. Configuring the AATOM model is the first step of the procedure. The well-defined AATOM can subsequently be used for simulation in order to generate simulation data for training and validating the surrogate model. The simulation data is pre-processed with the result that the surrogate model can achieve better performance. It consists of defining the relevant parameter values and re-sampling the simulation data to better train the surrogate model. Pre-processing is performed after the first iteration of generating the surrogate model. The following step is training the Random Forest. The training data-set is provided from the simulation data of the second step. The simulation data is randomly divided into two thirds for training data-set and one third for validation data-set [19]. The fifth step, the evaluation of the surrogate model, is subdivided into the validation of the surrogate model and a scenario-based evaluation. The last step is the comparison of the two surrogate models.

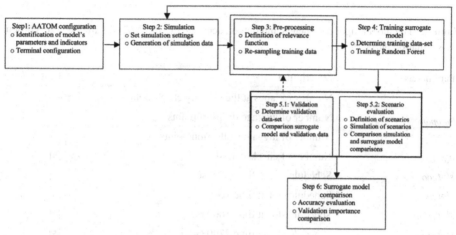

Fig. 1. The schematic representation of the methodology for obtaining a trained surrogate model based on AATOM.

The AATOM has a modular architecture, which requires a specific configuration for simulating airport terminal operations. In Fig. 2, the chosen configuration for conducting the surrogate model generation is visually represented. The model consists of a check-in and security checkpoint with each having a queuing system in place. Moreover, the gate area is included in the model. The defined model parameters and indicators. Both are given in Table 1. The input parameters in Table 1 represents a one hour flight schedule, with the first time slot scheduled 400 s after the start of the hour and the last slot scheduled 3400 s after the start. Each slot is assigned either zero (if no flight is scheduled) or the number of passengers for the scheduled flight. Furthermore, regarding the output given in Table 1, both queuing time and throughput for security checkpoint and check-in are included. For both the training and validation data-set, relatively large pool of sample points is drawn from simulation using the Latin Hypercube sampling method [20].

The surrogate model, given a combination of input values, is required to predict the values of the output variables. However, the accuracy of the surrogate model may differ for the different target variables. It is possible that the surrogate is unable to achieve the validity criteria for one or multiple target variables. There exist different strategies for coping with it [21, 22]. The strategy used in this research is the utility-based regression and re-sampling approach. The training data points consist of value combination of inputs and outputs as defined in Table 1. For the Random Forest model, several hyperparameters need to be determined prior to the training such as the number of trees and the number

Fig. 2. The AATOM layout including the check-in, security, and gate ([Janssen 2020]).

Table 1. The model input parameters and output, according to the AATOM architecture, chosen for simulation purpose.

Parameters	Description	Unit
n_{lanes}	Number of lanes at the security check-point	–
$n_{dropoff}$	Number of luggage drop-off points	–
$n_{collect}$	Number of luggage collection points	–
n_{desks}	Number of check-in desks	[s]
$slot_{400}$	Schedule slot at time 400 (sec)	[s]
$slot_{1000}$	Schedule slot at time 1000 (sec)	[s]
$slot_{1600}$	Schedule slot at time 1600 (sec)	[s]
$slot_{2200}$	Schedule slot at time 2200 (sec)	[s]
$slot_{2800}$	Schedule slot at time 2800 (sec)	[s]
$slot_{3400}$	Schedule slot at time 3400 (sec)	[s]
Output		
$scQueue_{avg}$	Average security checkpoint queuing time	[s]
$checkinQueue_{avg}$	Average check-in queuing time	[s]
$throughput_{checkin}$	Number of passengers that passed the check-in	[s]
$throughput_{sc}$	Number of passengers that passed the checkpoint	–
$TimeToGate_{avg}$	Average time to the gate	[s]
$n_{missedFlights}$	Number of missed flights	–

of sample points drawn for each tree. For the purpose of the research, the Bayesian optimization algorithm has been chosen for tuning hyperparameters, proven to be reliable and efficiently applied in previous studies [23, 24].

Lastly, subsequent to training the surrogate model, validating the model is required. The output indicators of the AATOM on the validation set are compared with the outputs from the validation set using the Mean Absolute Percentage Error (MAPE). From literature [19], Random Forest surrogate models often achieve accuracies of more than 90%. The scenario evaluation is based on a set of scenarios that represent real-world airport terminal cases that are given in Table 2. The scenario is a combination of a set of resources, related to the check-in a checkpoint, and a given (one hour) flight schedule. Three different scenarios in Table 2 represents three different levels of passenger demand: low demand (LOW), medium demand (MED) and high demand (HIGH). The levels are based on a regular flight schedule at Rotterdam-The Hague Airport (RTHA). In each scenario, the fixed resource allocation is based on prior research analyzing check-in and checkpoint systems in the context of airport security [1, 25]. One security checkpoint lane has an approximate capability of 160 passenger per hour and one check-in desk is able to process on average 60 passengers per hour. The flight schedules are derived from the flight schedule of RTHA, having on a peak hour an average of six flights scheduled. The representation is an hour of time slots where the value indicates the number of passengers scheduled for that time slot (empty if no flight is scheduled). Moreover, the number of passengers correspond to the Boeing 737 and 738 that are common aircraft at RTHA.

Table 2. The set of scenarios for fixed resource allocation for the different flight schedules, with four resource variables (n_{lanes}, n_{drop}, $n_{collect}$, $n_{checkin}$) and six time slots (from 400 to 3400).

ID	Resource allocation				Flight schedule					
	n_{lanes}	n_{drop}	$n_{collect}$	$n_{checkin}$	400	1000	1600	2200	2800	3400
LOW	3	3	3	7	186			186		
MED	5	3	3	12	197		142	197		164
HIGH	7	3	3	19	186	197	186	142	197	197

The methodology proposed for analyzing the sensitivity of the agent-based model using the surrogate neural network model, consists of two phases. In the first phase, the security checkpoint parameters of the AATOM are used as an input for the neural network. The influence of each parameter's uncertainty on the output uncertainty is determined through a series of forced perturbations on the parameters. The variation of the six parameters of interest, and in the second phase, the result of changes with respect to the variation of each parameter is considered for the output layer in the neural network. The training and validation of the neural network for the prediction part are performed, and eventually, the value of the weight from each input is considered as the importance of that parameter. To measure the sensitivity of each parameter such as average queue time in the security check-point, we have used the method proposed in [17].

The range of parameter values are based on standard values for RTHA are given in Table 3. The $n_{flights}$ are divided into time of scheduling and number of passengers. It can take the following values: [0, 142, 153, 164, 175, 186, 197]. Both time slots are combined in an array, e.g. [[1600, 142], [3400, 142]]. The value ranges for the other parameters are determined by the limitation of the simulation model.

4   Results

In this Section results are presented, using the methodology described in Sect. 3. The evaluation results comprise validation using simulation data and scenarios, with the

Table 3. Value ranges of the AATOM parameters for training.

AATOM parameter	Range
n_{lanes}	[1, 2, 3, 4, 5, 6, 7, 8]
$n_{dropoff}$	[1, 2, 3]
$n_{collect}$	[1, 2, 3]
n_{desks}	[1, 2, 3, 4, 5, 6, 7, 8, 9, 10, 11, 12]
$n_{flights}$	[1, 2, 3, 4, 5, 6]

evaluation given in Table 4. It contains the time performance and accuracy measurements for both the Random Forest model and the ANN model. From Table 4, the Random Forest model has a low training and execution time. Regarding the measured using MAPE accuracy, the overall performance of the Random Forest model is attaining values of 90% and above, with an average accuracy of 92.90%. Moreover, the most accurate prediction, being the *TimeToGate*, is reaching 97.13%. It can be explained by considering that the *TimeToGate* is the indicator based on the most information contained in the simulation model. Nonetheless, the indicator for the number of missed flights is less accurately predicted, only achieving 83.44% accuracy.

Table 4. Comparison of performances between the random forest surrogate model and the artificial neural network surrogate model.

Performances indicator	RF	ANN
Training time [sec]	3.82	12.54
Execution time [sec]	0.12	0.91
Mean absolute percentage error		
$scQueue_{avg}$	96.02%	94.39%
$checkinQueue_{avg}$	91.66%	93.71%
$throughput_{checkin}$	94.71%	91.29%
$throughput_{sc}$	94.44%	95.61%
$TimeToGate_{avg}$	97.13%	98.81%
$n_{missedFlights}$	83.41%	80.12%
Mean accuracy	92.90%	93.87%

Furthermore, comparing the Random Forest and ANN model, it can be seen that the ANN model is slower on both the training and execution time. However, the ANN model is still largely faster than the AATOM. On the accuracy, both models have similar performances. The *TimeToGate* is also the most accurate prediction for the ANN model. Lastly, the same difference between the accuracy of the $n_{missedFlights}$ and the other indicators is present in the ANN case, only reaching 80.12%. Successively, the second evaluation is given in Table 5. The accuracy of the surrogate model is given for each indicator at every level of passenger demand. First, the model has on overall poor performance on the LOW scenario compared to the two other scenarios, with the largest differences on the accuracy for the two checkpoint indicators and the $n_{missedFlights}$. The most apparent reason is the lack of training data sampled around the region of the variable values defined in the LOW scenario. The *TimeToGate* performance is a direct consequence of the poor performance on the checkpoint indicators, measuring the behavior.

Table 5. The prediction for different scenarios from the trained RF surrogate model.

ID	$checkinQueue_{avg}$	$scQueue_{avg}$	$TimeToGate_{avg}$	$n_{missedFlights}$	$throughput_{checkin}$	$throughput_{sc}$
LOW	89.13%	60.56%	80.01%	0%	94.1%	75.88%
MED	93.58%	88.62%	92.64%	8.81%	92.82%	98.21%
HIGH	88.17%	94.95%	95.38%	61.53%	91.45%	94.94%

Furthermore, the surrogate model's low accuracy on the $n_{missedFlights}$ is also visible in the results of the two other scenarios. There is a visible increase in accuracy with increasing passenger demand, growing from 0% to 61.53%. Moreover, the surrogate model was trained on a wide range of cases with highly varying $n_{missedFlights}$ values. Additional insight is given into the underlying relationships between the parameters and indicators of the original model (the AATOM). The first analysis is the measure of importance of the different variables. The variable importance measure (VIM) is calculated for both surrogate models (Random Forest and ANN), given in Fig. 3. As can be seen in Fig. 3(a), there are two distinct variables, identified by VIM as the most important variables: the number of lanes of the security checkpoint and the number of desks at the check-in. Both variables are regulating the processing capacity of passengers at the two systems (checkpoint and check-in), therefore the indication from the VIM conforms with the representation of the two variables in the airport terminal operations. Moreover, from Fig. 3(a), the four resource allocation variables (n_{lanes}, $n_{dropoff}$, $n_{collect}$, n_{desks}) are relatively more important than the flight schedule variables (time-slots). All indicators, except for the $n_{missedFlights}$, are measuring time performance through queueing or throughput. Hence, the resource allocation is more directly related to the time performance of the terminal than the flight schedule, dictating the check-in and checkpoint behavior. The last observation in Fig. 3(a) is the trend of the time-slot importance, with the first and last slot being the least important slots. Presumably, the importance of the middle slots stems from the effect of reducing the time between flights by adding more slots in the scheduling hour. The VIM of the ANN model is given in Fig. 3(b) for comparison purposes with the RF model. Multiple similarities are perceivable between the two models, with the most recognizable that the same two most important variables (n_{desks} and n_{lanes}) are identified with the VIM. Additionally, the resource allocation variables are prominently more important than the flight time-slots. Besides, there are several differences between the RF model's VIM and the ANN model's VIM. First, the importance measure difference between the two most important variables is lower. The lower difference is possibly due to the use of a different surrogate model, hence both models are not using the variable information in exactly the same manner to make predictions on the different target variables. Second, the ranking of the collect and drop-off location variables is reversed. Nonetheless, the order of magnitude is similar for both variables in both models.

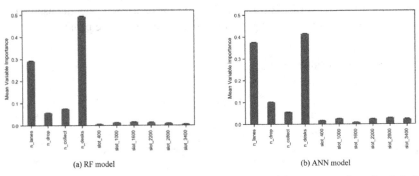

(a) RF model   (b) ANN model

Fig. 3. The variable importance measure for the AATOM model parameters from the default RF and the ANN surrogate model

Furthermore, an analysis of the surrogate model accuracy is given by systematically adding variables to the model. At each addition the predictions made by the surrogate model are compared with the validation data-set. The different mean accuracy levels obtained for both models are given in Table 6. Figure 4 visualizes the accuracy change by adding model variables. From Table 6 and Fig. 4, it can be seen that the four resource variables are supporting the RF model to make predictions with an averaged accuracy of 86.82%. Adding the remaining variables increases the mean accuracy by 6%. Hence, clearly observable in Fig. 4, the resource allocation variables have the largest contribution to the increase in prediction accuracy of the surrogate model. For the RF model, there is the small reduction of accuracy after the addition of the first time-slot variable. However, the difference is sufficiently small (0.07%) to be neglected. Furthermore, by comparing the RF and ANN model in Table 6, several similarities can be observed. First, the resource variables are sufficient for the ANN model to reach an accuracy of 89.77%. The remaining variables, similar to the RF model, are only slightly increasing the prediction accuracy by 4%. Second, the most important variable is the n_{desks}, related to similar VIM. Nonetheless, there is an observable difference between the contribution of the time-slot variables in the RF model and the ANN model. The differences coincide with the VIM of the variables in Fig. 3. As mentioned earlier, the $n_{missedFlights}$ is the one target variable for which the surrogate model experiences difficulties to make accurate predictions. The accuracy is lower for the specific scenarios than for an evaluation based on the validation data. In essence, the nature of the $n_{missedFlights}$ is different from all other indicators of the AATOM simulation. All other indicators are measuring the efficiency in time or passenger count of the check-in and/or checkpoint. The $n_{missedFlights}$ is not directly explained by the dynamics of either of the systems, i.e. check-in or security checkpoint. This target variable is more evenly dependent on all the operational elements in the airport terminal. This can be observed in the VIM for predicting the $n_{missedFlights}$ and the incremental accuracy by variable addition, given in Fig. 5.

Table 6. The different mean accuracy levels obtained for RF and ANN surrogate models.

ID	Parameters	Included parameters	RF	ANN
1	n_{lanes}	[1]	62.53%	68.03%
2	$n_{dropoff}$	[1, 2]	65.50%	72.24%
3	$n_{collect}$	[1, 2, 3]	70.97%	76.91%
4	n_{desks}	[1, 2, 3, 4]	86.82%	89.77%
5	$slot_{400}$	[1, 2, 3, 4, 5]	87.75%	90.01%
1	$slot_{1000}$	[1, 2, 3, 4, 5, 6]	87.74%	90.80%
2	$slot_{1600}$	[1, 2, 3, 4, 5, 6, 7]	89.89%	92.26%
3	$slot_{2200}$	[1, 2, 3, 4, 5, 6, 7, 8]	91.32%	92.89%
4	$slot_{2800}$	[1, 2, 3, 4, 5, 6, 7, 8, 9]	92.38%	93.15%
5	$slot_{3400}$	[1, 2, 3, 4, 5, 6, 7, 8, 9, 10]	92.88%	93.76%

According to Fig. 5(a), the n_{lanes} is the most important variable. The average time to check a passenger at a checkpoint lane is higher than for the check-in. Hence, the number of lanes present at the checkpoint largely determine the number of passengers that can arrive on time for the flight. Furthermore, from Fig. 5(a), the importance of all remaining variables is approximately evenly distributed. Thus, it indicates the necessity of all variable information to achieve adequate accuracy (above 80%) on the validation data. The figure depicts the change in accuracy by step-wise addition of the variables. In contrast with the same plot from Fig. 4, the accuracy is linearly increasing with every variable addition.

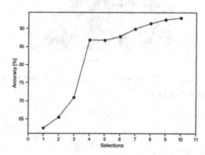

Fig. 4. The model accuracy with addition of variables from the RF surrogate model.

Moreover, the surrogate model is predicting less accurately the smaller number of missed flights. The chosen measure for accuracy (MAPE) determines the absolute differences between the prediction of the surrogate model and the simulation result.

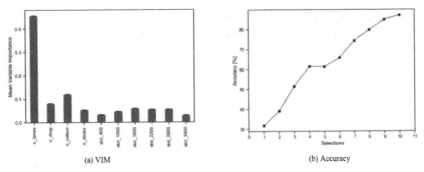

(a) VIM   (b) Accuracy

Fig. 5. The variable importance and model accuracy with addition of variables from the RF surrogate model for predicting the number of missed flights.

Hence, for smaller numbers of $n_{missedFlights}$ the difference in percentage are larger, for example predicting 4 instead of 6 reveals an inaccuracy of 40%. Second, the number of missed flights occurring over the flight hour schedule is a rare event, especially rare for the lower values. The infrequent occurrence complicates the task of training and predicting this indicator. Last, the range of values for the $n_{missedFlights}$ is wide, visualized in Fig. 6. Hence, it is more complex for the surrogate model to achieve high accuracy on the whole spectrum. However, utility-based regression and the method for re-sampling, did not improve the accuracy of the surrogate model. The method has been applied on re-sampling the data to under-sample the higher values of the number of missed flights.

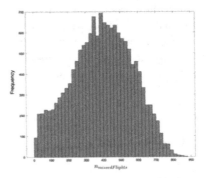

Fig. 6. Distribution of the $n_{missedFlihgts}$ from the dataset, with the number of missed flights over the number of occurrences in the dataset.

5 Discussion and Conclusion

The research purpose was to study an approach for using an approximation of the AATOM in order to make predictions on the behavior of airport terminal operations in a computationally efficient manner. The study included two additional aspects: preserving the properties of the original model and getting an insight in the underlying dynamics of the AATOM. The method consists of an iterative process in which the AATOM generates simulation data for training and validation of the surrogate model. The surrogate model used in the method is a random forest model. The trained surrogate model was evaluated based on the absolute difference between the model predictions and the simulations results from the validation data-set. An additional evaluation was made on specific scenarios for different levels of passenger demands. Furthermore, an additional surrogate model was developed for comparison, based on ANN. The ANN model is also evaluated on the validation data-set and provided additional insight on the underlying relationships in the AATOM. Regarding the approximation, the obtained the RF-based surrogate model is able to make accurate predictions on all indicators except one, the number of missed flights. It achieves an average accuracy of 93%. For the number of missed flights, the accuracy is reaching 83%. Further analysis highlights the wide range of number of missed flights simulated and the difficulty for the surrogate to make accurate predictions on the lower numbers. Moreover, the evaluation on the scenarios has shown the generalization capability of the surrogate model, with the same difficulty to make accurate predictions of the number of missed flights. The ANN model attains similar accuracy on all indicators and encounters the same issue with the predictions on the number of missed flights. In general, the results have shown through accuracy evaluation that the emergent properties, represented by the model indicators, are preserved by achieving acceptable accuracy levels.

References

1. Janssen, S., Sharpanskykh, A., Curran, R.: Agent-based modelling and analysis of security and efficiency in airport terminals. Transp. Res. Part C: Emerg. Technol. **100**, 142–160 (2019)
2. Janssen, S.: Capturing agents in security models: agent-based security risk management using causal discovery (2020)
3. Lee, J.-S., et al.: The complexities of agent-based modeling output analysis. J. Artif. Soc. Soc. Simul. **18**(4), 4 (2015)
4. Van der Hoog, S.: Surrogate modelling in (and of) agent-based models: a prospectus. Comput. Econ. **53**, 1245–1263 (2018). https://doi.org/10.1007/s10614-018-9802-0
5. Lamperti, F., Roventini, A., Sani, A.: Agent-based model calibration using machine learning surrogates. J. Econ. Dyn. Control **90**, 366–389 (2018)
6. Zhang, Y., Li, Z., Zhang, Y.: Validation and calibration of an agent-based model: a surrogate approach. Discret. Dyn. Nat. Soc. **2020**, 6946370 (2020)
7. Edali, M., Yücel, G.: Exploring the behavior space of agent-based simulation models using random forest metamodels and sequential sampling. Simul. Model. Pract. Theory **92**, 62–81 (2019)
8. Villa-Vialaneix, N., Follador, M., Ratto, M., Leip, A.: A comparison of eight metamodeling techniques for the simulation of N_2O fluxes and n leaching from corn crops. Environ. Model. Softw. **34**, 51–66 (2012)
9. Biau, G., Scornet, E.: A random forest guided tour. TEST **25**(2), 197–227 (2016). https://doi. org/10.1007/s11749-016-0481-7
10. Boulesteix, A., Janitza, S., Kruppa, J., König, I.R.: Overview of random forest methodology and practical guidance with emphasis on computational biology and bioinformatics. Wiley Interdiscip. Rev.: Data Min. Knowl. Disc. **2**(6), 493–507 (2012)
11. James, G., Witten, D., Hastie, T., Tibshirani, R.: An Introduction to Statistical Learning (2013)

12. Behnamian, A., Millard, K., Banks, S.N., White, L., Richardson, M., Pasher, J.: A systematic approach for variable selection with random forests: achieving stable variable importance values. IEEE Geosci. Remote Sens. Lett. **14**(11), 1988–1992 (2017)

13. Pedregosa, F., et al.: Scikit-learn: machine learning in Python. J. Mach. Learn. Res. **12**, 2825–2830 (2011)

14. Kira, K., Rendell, L.A.: The feature selection problem: traditional methods and a new algorithm. In: AAAI, vol. 2, pp. 129–134 (1992)

15. Garson, D.G.: Interpreting neural network connection weights (1991)

16. Goodfellow, I., Bengio, Y., Courville, A., Bengio, Y.: Deep Learning, vol. 1. MIT Press, Cambridge (2016)

17. Welford, B.: Note on a method for calculating corrected sums of squares and products. Technometrics **4**(3), 419–420 (1962)

18. Sadeghyan, S.: A new robust feature selection method using variance-based sensitivity analysis. arXiv preprint arXiv:1804.05092 https://arxiv.org/abs/1804.05092 (2018)

19. Kleijnen, J.P.C., Sargent, R.G.: A methodology for fitting and validating metamodels in simulation. Eur. J. Oper. Res. **120**(1), 14–29 (2000)

20. Kleijnen, J.P., Sanchez, S.M., Lucas, T.W., Cioppa, T.M.: State-of-the-art review: a user's guide to the brave new world of designing simulation experiments. INFORMS J. Comput. **17**(3), 263–289 (2005)

21. Branco, P., Torgo, L., Ribeiro, R.: A survey of predictive modelling under imbalanced distributions. arXiv preprint arXiv:1505.01658 https://arxiv.org/abs/1505.01658 (2015)

22. Torgo, L., Branco, P., Ribeiro, R.P., Pfahringer, B.: Resampling strategies for regression. Expert Syst. **32**(3), 465–476 (2015)

23. Bergstra, J., Bardenet, R., Bengio, Y., Kégl, B.: Algorithms for hyperparameter optimization. Adv. Neural. Inf. Process. Syst. **24**, 2546–2554 (2011)

24. Wu, J., Chen, X.-Y., Zhang, H., Xiong, L.-D., Lei, H., Deng, S.-H.: Hyperparameter optimization for machine learning models based on Bayesian optimization. J. Electron. Sci. Technol. **17**(1), 26–40 (2019)

25. Janssen, S., van der Sommen, R., Dilweg, A., Sharpanskykh, A.: Data-driven analysis of airport security checkpoint operations. Aerospace **7**(6), 69 (2020)

26. Mekić, A., Mohammadi Ziabari, S.S., Sharpanskykh, A.: Systemic agent-based modeling and analysis of passenger discretionary activities in airport terminals. Aerospace **8**(6), 162 (2021)

27. Ziabari, S., Sanders, G., Mekic, A., Sharpanskykh, A.: Demo paper: a tool for analyzing COVID-19-related measurements using agent-based support simulator for airport terminal operations. In: Dignum, F., Corchado, J.M., De La Prieta, F. (eds.) Advances in Practical Applications of Agents, Multi-Agent Systems, and Social Good, vol. 12946, pp. 359–362. Springer, Cham (2021). https://doi.org/10.1007/978-3-030-85739-4_32

28. Sanders, G., Mohammadi Ziabari, S.S., Mekić, A., Sharpanskykh, A.: Agent-based modelling and simulation of airport terminal operations under COVID-19-related restrictions. In: Dignum, F., Corchado, J.M., De La Prieta, F. (eds.) Advances in Practical Applications of Agents, Multi-Agent Systems, and Social Good, vol. 12946, pp. 214–228. Springer, Cham (2021). https://doi.org/10.1007/978-3-030-85739-4_18

School's Out? Simulating Schooling Strategies During COVID-19

Lukas Tapp[✉], Veronika Kurchyna, Falco Nogatz, Jan Ole Berndt,
and Ingo J. Timm

Smart Data & Knowledge Services, Cognitive Social Simulation, German Research
Center for Artificial Intelligence (DFKI), Kaiserslautern, Germany
{lukas.tapp,veronika.kurchyna,falco.nogatz,jan_ole.berndt,
ingo.timm}@dfki.de

Abstract. Multi-agent based systems offer the possibility to examine
the effects of policies down to specific target groups while also considering the effects on a population-level scale. To examine the impact of
different schooling strategies, an agent-based model is used in the context
of the COVID-19 pandemic using a German city as an example. The simulation experiments show that reducing the class size by rotating weekly
between in-person classes and online schooling is effective at preventing
infections while driving up the detection rate among children through
testing during weeks of in-person attendance. While open schools lead
to higher infection rates, a surprising result of this study is that school
rotation is almost as effective at lowering infections among both the student population and the general population as closing schools. Due to the
continued testing of attending students, the overall infections in the general population are even lower in a school rotation scenario, showcasing
the potential for emergent behaviors in agent-based models.

Keywords: COVID-19 simulation · Non-pharmaceutical intervention ·
Policy-making and evaluation

1 Introduction

Since the beginning of the COVID-19 pandemic in early 2020, policymakers
across the globe face a novel virus spreading at an unprecedented scale. Without
experience to rely on, governments often struggle to contain the spread of the
virus. Quickly, a flood of data and information became available to decision
makers on all levels of government. Infection rates in districts and counties,
unemployment statistics, the current strain on health systems and critical care
facilities, the financial impact of lockdowns and strict hygiene measures, social
media – a variety of input that must be considered when making decisions.

The researchers have advised policymakers in various German crisis response
groups using a novel dashboard, which approaches the current issues decision

F. Lorig and E. Norling (Eds.): MABS 2022, LNAI 13743, pp. 95–106, 2023.
https://doi.org/10.1007/978-3-031-22947-3_8

makers face from two angles: The dashboard offers a compact overview of important data from various sources, allowing policymakers to gain a faster understanding of the current situation. Additionally, the dashboard is connected to the agent-based *SoSAD model* (Social Simulation for Analysis of Infectious Disease Control) [18]. In this model, the inhabitants of a city are modeled as agents who follow their daily schedules and may spread the disease during interactions. The simulation model enables users to examine the anticipated effects of different non-pharmaceutical interventions such as mask mandates, mandated home office for workers, closing schools, or other measures that aim at reducing infectious contacts.

Analysing different strategies that allow handling the pandemic in schools is the main objective of the paper, based on the counseling work done in different crisis response groups. Since the closing of schools has a strong negative impact on the psychological and intellectual development of children [10], it is important to examine how to keep the number of students in schools at a high level while simultaneously avoiding high disease rates among students and its impact on the general population.

This paper discusses the modeling of infectious diseases with particular focus on uses for policy-making in Sect. 2 before presenting the approach of the SoSAD model in Sect. 3 and how it was used to examine different schooling strategies in Sect. 4. First promising simulation results are presented in Sect. 5, followed by an evaluation of the model itself in Sect. 6. Finally, in Sect. 7, we discuss future work and conclude. After all, this work also explains why this use case is a prime example of the usefulness of agent-based models (ABM) in policy-making contexts.

2   Agent-Based Models in the Pandemic

To predict future behavior in context of pandemics, different simulation studies were conducted since the beginning of the pandemic [11]. Most used a traditional mathematical macro-scale approach [16]. However, many were not capable of simulating social and behavioral factors, such as individual response to countermeasures or social relationships like families living together in a household [17]. ABMs are better suited to express the complexity between individuals. Within multi-agent based systems, many approaches choose a network model in which diseases spread along connections between agents, centering the simulation around relationships. However, this approach doesn't consider that infection chains are often hard to trace [3], as people don't have a static set of people to interact with. Further, such network models have a reduced capacity for implementing individual measures that are specific to certain locations, such as vaccine mandates at workplaces, reduced contact rates, and the closing of schools.

While policymakers have no access to the decision-making and relationships of people, they can influence the behavior of people by setting rules and limitations for the locations where possibly infectious contacts take place, such as leisure activities, workplaces, and schools. As such, it is important to examine a model that allows for different strategies in locations with an agent model that models spatial networks.

There's a number of models that present an ABM to simulate infectious diseases such as COVID-19 and also include students and schools [11]. Many of these models, such as [7], only distinguish between open or closed schools without compromise solutions such as school rotation. In models such as [4], synthetic populations are used to examine different modes of school operations in combination with face-mask adherence. The number of students can be halved permanently, but students do not rotate weekly, which has different implications for the actual contact behaviors. In [13], a model is presented to examine the loss of schooling days due to school closures during the COVID-19 pandemic. Different strategies, such as reducing teacher-student ratios or the use of school rotation, are examined here. However, this model only considers households and a single school with multiple classes, which deviates from reality, where students attend different schools and interact across households, schools and classes during leisure activities.

Due to the desired flexibility in the range of questions that can be answered, we chose to use the SoSAD modeling approach, which allows for the simulation of different non-pharmaceutical interventions, spatial networks that support location-based policies and the inclusion of real-world data.

3   The SoSAD Modeling Approach

The SoSAD modeling approach aims towards flexibility and extensibility to allow swift response to new demands and developments. In the following sections, an overview of the key concepts will be given, starting with the modeling of the population and infrastructure, the activities and contacts during which contagion can take place and the countermeasures supported by the model. The conceptual behavior of the agents is described, while the implementation of the mechanisms around routines, interactions and contagions is displayed in Fig. 1 in a simplified manner focused on the activities of agents.

3.1   Population and Infrastructure

The agents are modeled after the general population of a German city with approximately 100.000 inhabitants. Thanks to the close cooperation with the city's local government, the researchers have access to anonymized data that provides information about the structure of households, schools and city districts. Each agent in SoSAD represents an individual person of a particular age. Depending on their age, these agents are clustered into three distinct behavioral groups: children (including adolescents), workers (including university students), and pensioners (i.e., all agents above the age of retirement). The population consists of a total of 102798 agents, of which 15888 are students, 67169 are workers and 19741 are pensioners. The infrastructure of the model consists of several locations, such as households, leisure activities, workplaces and schools

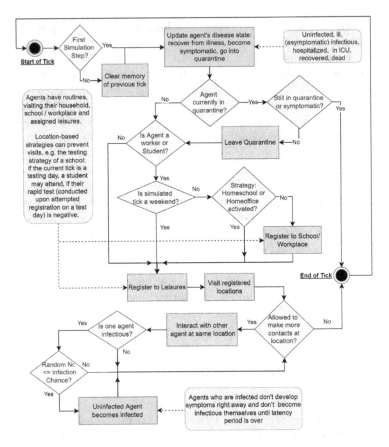

Fig. 1. The SoSAD modeling approach: Decision-making of agents for daily activities. The rounded squares provide additional information about further mechanisms.

as well as hospitals with attached intensive care units to include the pandemic's impact on the healthcare system. In total, 56663 households, 175 leisure activities, 175 workplaces and 33 schools with 400 classes are represented within the model. The number of households, schools and classes is based on official data.

Agents and locations form a dynamic bipartite graph. This graph determines which agents can encounter and possibly infect each other at which location. The locations an agent frequents are determined by its daily routines defined during initialisation. Workers have a workplace which can represent a private company, a public service agency, as well as a university or other facilities. All agents under the age of 18 attend schools. Agents of any age have a household where they live alone or with other agents, depending on the population data. Furthermore, all agent's frequent leisure facilities which represent shops as suppliers of both essential and non-essential goods as well as cinemas, gyms, stadiums, and concert halls as well as any other public places for recreational activities. While not considered in this paper, special locations and infrastructure, such as school busses and public swimming pools, have been implemented and analyzed by request of the city to investigate the possible impact of policy decisions.

3.2   Contacts and Contagion

Agents frequenting the same location may come into contact with each other. Contacts are randomly chosen from the pool of visitors, based on the permitted number of contacts that can be made in this location type. Interactions are reciprocal, assuring no agents exceed their allowed contact numbers. Since not every encounter will be potentially contagious, the model only considers contacts that were sufficiently intense in duration and proximity for a contagion. If a contagious agent encounters a currently uninfected but vulnerable agent, there is a percentage probability to infect the healthy agent based on the infectiousness of the modeled disease. This is the same basic principle as in most other agent-based contagion models [11]. These settings can be defined individually for each agent group in our model. Spatial factors, such as distance, time, indoors or outdoors, as well as particle dynamics, are not explicitly considered. Infection chances follow estimated average transmission probabilities for typical activities at particular locations.

The model of disease states and their progression is analogous to a modified SEIR approach as published by the Robert Koch-Institute, the German government's central scientific institution for biomedicine and public health [2]. Any agent that has not yet been infected with the virus is susceptible to it (state S). If the virus is transmitted to such an agent, that agent becomes exposed (E). After a latency period, the agent becomes infectious for a period (I) during which it can infect other agents it encounters. In the case of COVID-19, an agent becomes infectious before it may develop symptoms of illness (i.e., the latency period is shorter than the incubation period). There are six levels of symptoms, one of which is predefined for each agent: asymptomatic, mild, moderate, severe, critical, and fatal. Asymptomatic agents are not aware of their disease state. Mild infections are not necessarily recognized as an infection with COVID-19 and an agent may continue going about their schedules despite minor symptoms [5]. Moderate symptoms mean that the agent may or must stay at home until it recovers, thereby having no further contacts with other agents at work, school, or leisure facilities. However, these agents will still interact with any other agent living in their household. Agents with severe or critical symptoms will be hospitalised, possibly with intensive care, and will not have any contacts during their stay. Agents with a fatal level of severity pass away and are removed from the model. Recovered agents will become (partially) immunized to further infection (R). Due to recent findings in the pandemic [1,9,15], recovery will decrease the reinfection chance of partially immunized agents and further assure that if a recovered agent is reinfected, their disease will be of decreased severity.

3.3   Activities and Countermeasures

Without any countermeasures to combat the spread of the virus, the disease will keep spreading repeatedly, although hypothetically, after a sufficient number of infections, any agent should either pass away or become fully immune. However, in reality, agents and (local) government and businesses will impose restrictions on the behavior of agents to slow down and reduce the infection dynamics.

The SoSAD model offers the following strategies and measures to influence the rate at which infections spread in the model: by forcing symptomatically ill patients into quarantine, the spread of the virus can be restricted to household members only, where infection is not necessarily guaranteed due to different living circumstances. By reducing the leisure contacts for both adults and children, infections can be reduced. This includes customer limits in stores, mandatory hygiene concepts at leisure facilities and reduced contacts with friends or family.

Once vaccines became widely available, Germany implemented the so-called '3G-Strategy': vaccinated, recovered, or tested (Geimpft, Genesen, Getestet). Only individuals with a valid vaccination, proven recovery or recent test result may access leisure activities such as restaurants, sport events and similar. Towards Winter 2021, the strategy was narrowed down to the two variants '2G', which no longer accepted unvaccinated and unrecovered individuals regardless of test results, as well as '2G Plus' which required a recent test result on top of vaccination or recovery certificate. These strategies are also present in the SoSAD model, allowing to account for the effects of such strategies on the infection dynamics at leisure activities and workplaces. While not all industries allow for the same degree of remote work, increasing the home office rate among the working population also helps reducing contacts in the workplace. In Fall 2021, Germany saw an estimated home office rate of about 20 % [8] due to the accelerating infection dynamics.

In the same vein, homeschooling is another means of reducing contacts among children, either by fully closing schools or by having a certain percentage of children being homeschooled. School Rotation is a special form of schooling, in which classes are split in half and have students taking turns between in-person classes and online lessons. Another means of reducing the disease spread in schools is regular testing of students using rapid tests and the quarantine of students who were tested positive, along with classmates who have frequent contacts with them. Finally, schools with offset start times help reducing possibly infectious contacts among students on their way to school, given that public transportation may frequently be crowded. Social distancing cannot be guaranteed in such cases.

4   Simulating Three Schooling Strategies

In our analysis of schooling strategies, the following three options were simulated and evaluated:

(i) *Regular schooling with reduced contacts:* In this case, the regular class and course cohorts in the schools are taught completely as in normal operation. Distance rules can only be observed to a limited extent during lessons (depending on the room capacity). Therefore, mouth and nose protection are also worn during lessons and the room is aired regularly. The cohorts remain separated as much as possible during break times. However, complete separation is also not possible because of school bus traffic, so that infections may also occur across cohorts.

(ii) *Closed Schools:* In this case, there is no attendance at the schools. The schools are therefore eliminated as a site of possible infections.

(iii) *Rotation of halved classes (school rotation):* In this case, the class or course cohorts are divided in half. One half is taught in face-to-face classes and the other half is taught at home. The change takes place weekly. All other measures according to strategy (i) remain in effect here as well. Since less students meet on their way to school and less space is taken in the classes and other areas in school, contacts and infections among students are expected to be lower compared to schools operating at their usual capacity.

While different scenarios regarding the virus variant, contact rates and other circumstances have been simulated, this paper presents the results of a simulation study conducted using a highly infectious variant of COVID-19 inspired by the novel Omicron strain which causes skyrocketing infection cases in many countries. To model the high infectiousness of the Omicron variant [6], the model assumes the virus to be twice as infectious as the Delta variant and an increased reinfection rate of 50 %, meaning that initially vaccinated people are no longer considered to be fully immune. In December 2021, researchers were not yet certain about the effectiveness of vaccinations against the new strain [6], inspiring the choice to set initial vaccinations to 0 % to examine the impact of schooling strategy decisions in a worst-case scenario. The other parameters were calibrated using simulated annealing. Several configurations were able to replicate real world data. However, some combinations, such as very high leisure contacts for adults, contradict existing research [12] and thus, the authors chose a configuration that is consistent with empirical findings. In all three scenarios, the initial state is based on the month of December 2021 in Germany, based on official data provided by the RKI during that time period [14].

Due to the relatively low infection numbers in the model city over the course of the pandemic, the infections prior to the start of the simulation are based on reports of the corresponding federal state adjusted for the smaller population size. Due to the pandemic, reduced contact rates of agents are assumed compared to a non-pandemic [12]. Both private and professional contacts of adults are set to an average of two contacts per day. For students, a higher number of leisure and school contacts is assumed (number of contacts: 3 per day) [12]. This is partially due to the fact that in school buildings, space is often too limited to allow for effective social distancing. To ensure the safety of students, frequent tests are conducted to filter out infected students as early as possible. In this experiment setup, students attending school are tested twice in a 5-day-school week (on Monday and Thursday) using a rapid test. In case of a positive result, either due to infection or a false positive, the student is quarantined. This simplified testing strategy will be employed for any student attending school on testing days in

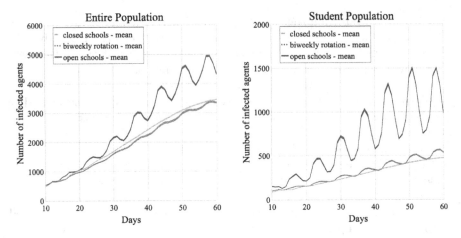

Fig. 2. Absolute number of active infections among the entire population (left) and students (right) with confidence interval (95 %). Measured average of 100 runs.

both the open school and school rotation scenarios. The home office rate for workers and university students is rounded to an estimated 20 % of the working age population working from home.

The only variation between the three scenarios lies in the schooling strategies. For the school rotation scenario, the school contacts are additionally reduced to 2 to express the fact that fewer students attend school. This leads to easier social distancing in classrooms, fewer individuals using public transportation and splitting of social groups. In both open schools and school rotation, testing is applied as described above. The three scenarios were run with 100 different random seeds over 60 ticks each, only varying the parameters regarding the schooling strategies. The ticks represent one day within the simulation. The first ten ticks are considered a warm-up period in which the model initializes based on input data regarding infections among different cohorts at start. Thus, these first ten ticks were discarded and removed from the evaluation.

5   Can We Keep Schools Open? Simulation Results

To examine the impact of the three proposed schooling strategies, the number of infected agents was plotted both on the level of the general population as well as on student-level only. Figure 2 depicts the impact of the schooling strategies on the entire population (left) and students (right): Students may become sick in all scenarios, but both school rotation and the closing of schools are effective at reducing infections.

Depending on the strategy, the graphs represent a wave-shaped infection curve. The local minima represent weekends when there are fewer infectious encounters between agents due to the lack of professional contacts (workplace contacts and school contacts).

A surprising result of this study is that school rotation appears to be even more effective at lowering infections among the general population than closed schools. When schools remain open, students may become infected by their peers and carry this infection into their households, leading to higher infection rates, while the closing of schools prevents these contacts altogether. While the superiority of the school rotation may seem surprising at first, it can be explained with the fact that in a closed school scenario, students will still keep having leisure contacts and may become exposed to the virus by working parents. As children continue attending school every other week, they are tested regularly, leading to a higher detection and quarantine rate of infectious cases. The increased rate of detection and quarantine within the cohort of students, which is reflected in the infection rate of the entire population, can also be described as an emergent effect. This result is confirmed when considering the accumulated new infections in this model: when schools remain open, a mean of 30,147 individuals becomes infected with the virus. When schools are closed, only 23,512 agents become infected on average during the simulation time. In comparison to that, school rotation proves narrowly superior with only 22,401 infections on average during the simulation. Thus, the numbers confirm the conclusion drawn from the visualisations. While the difference between closed schools and school rotation strategies is small in terms of total infection numbers, it is important to remember that studies have proven the negative effects of closed schools [10], meaning that school rotation may provide a compromise solution.

The choice of schooling strategies has a strong impact on both the overall population and the student population. As the results show, reducing school operations alone is not sufficient to contain the pandemic. Still, students in particular benefit from the change in school strategy from open schools to school rotation without having to close the school entirely. Switching to school rotation also has the advantage that students are additionally tested when they attend school. Infected students can therefore be detected and quarantined, preventing further infections during leisure activities. When considering the entire population, alternating operation is even superior to school closure. This result showcases the special characteristic of ABMs: the ability to discover patterns that emerge from a combination of mechanisms without explicit modeling.

6   Discussion – Patterns in Different Experiment Setups

While only the results of one simulation experiment setup were discussed, more experiments were conducted in the past months when advising various crisis response groups. The most important takeaway of these simulation studies is the pattern shown above: school rotation shows a similar effectiveness in reducing infections as closing schools, as well as flattening the wavy behavior of the open school infection graphs.

In December 2021, during the first observation of the novel Omicron variant, different worst-case scenarios regarding the infectiousness and immune escape potential of the Omicron variant were examined. Even when the traits of the virus were greatly exaggerated compared to the observations in the real world, the general pattern of infection-mitigating effects of school rotation held up. Further experiments in the middle of December 2021, examining the effects of various lockdown scenarios over Christmas and New Year's, confirmed the same result patterns. In the lockdown scenario, in addition to switching the school strategies, other measures were considered, such as company vacations, various home office rates as well as contact restrictions. Other experimental setups in which the effect could be reproduced include combining the strategies with different home office rates, different vaccination rates, and with different COVID-19 variants, such as the original variant, Delta and possible variations of Omicron based on first published and rumored estimations. The positive effect of the school rotation on the entire population as well as on the students themselves can be reproduced.

As mentioned above, several parameter configurations were found that replicate infection patterns matching real world observations, including some that match further empirical findings. Therefore the model is generally plausible in its ability to produce realistic behavior. Overall, the model still needs further testing and validation. Calibration has shown that the model is generally capable of producing realistic behavior, which lends some level of credence to the results and trends shown up in the simulation studies. Given the setup of the experiments in which other parameters, such as contact rates, home office strategies among adults and even disease traits, have shown consistent patterns, school rotation appears to have positive effects on the population and students both. These effects are robust to parameter changes, though it is still up to decision makers to determine whether the difference between closed and school rotation operations is acceptable in the given situation.

Systematic real-life experiments between schooling strategies would be the best means of validating the model, but such experiments are not practically feasible due to ethical reasons. Further, since governments typically present several measures at the same time, it is difficult to separate the effects of different combinations into the contributions of individual policy decisions to compare the three different strategies. In such situations, sufficiently plausible and realistic simulations can help distinguishing the effects of strategies and attributing observations to individual measures.

7   Conclusion – What only ABMs Can Show

This paper presented an agent-based model to simulate the spread of a disease in a population. In this case, the model refers to the COVID-19 virus, which is spread when agents interact in different locations such as households, workplaces, schools and leisure activities. This model is used to simulate and analyze different schooling strategies to slow down and reduce infections among students. The experiments compared the impact of open schools with closed schools and school rotation, in which classes are halved and take weekly turns between in-person attendance and online schooling. The experiments have shown that school rotation is not only superior to open schools in terms of preventing infections, but even comparable to closed schools and may outperform the closed school strategy on a population level due to continued monitoring and quarantining of infected students through regular testing.

Schools are often said to not have a major impact on the infection dynamics across the entire population, but it is still important to prevent harm from children, a vulnerable demographic. Given the need to balance different interests, ABMs can help making such decisions – while both working parents and children would certainly favor open schools, it may be possible to reach a point in which keeping the schools open is considered an irresponsible decision. As such, the school rotation strategy prevents schools shutting down completely. A statistical model might have predicted that school rotation strategies offer a compromise between leaving schools open or closing them, but ABMs are superior in their ability to express the impact of an intervention on specific population groups. The key difference between statistical models and ABMs is the possibility to model individual activities, household structures and dynamic contact graphs. Infections can spread non-uniformly, leading to emergent behavior showcased in the results of this paper.

Without an ABM, the effects of school rotation would likely be dismissed entirely, given that the benefits and drawbacks of some approaches are difficult to conceptualize. Emergent behaviors such as this are often difficult to anticipate. The positive effect of school rotation on detection and quarantine further emphasizes the value of such complex models, given that a simpler model without different locations, agent groups and strategies would not have the capacity to show such emergent effects. Therefore, the authors believe that ABMs are a valuable tool in policy-making not just in the pandemic, but in any situation in which some decisions may show only little effects on a large scale but important impact on specific population groups which may be overlooked otherwise. In the future, the model will be extended by further components and also further validated. For this purpose, additional cities will be integrated into the model to test the model behavior in relation to other structural and demographic circumstances and the transferability to cities with different population and infrastructure.

Acknowledgement. This model was created in the context of *AScore*, a consortium project funded from 01/2021 until 12/2021 within the special program "Zivile Sicherheit - Forschungsansätze zur Aufarbeitung der Corona-Pandemie" by the German Federal Ministry of Education and Research (BMBF) under grant number 13N15663.

References

1. Abu-Raddad, L.J., et al.: Severity of SARS-CoV-2 reinfections as compared with primary infections. N. Engl. J. Med. **385**(26), 2487–2489 (2021). https://doi.org/10.1056/NEJMc2108120
2. Buchholz, U., et al.: Modellierung von Beispielszenarien der SARS-CoV-2-Ausbreitung und Schwere in Deutschland (2020)

3. Chowdhury, M.J.M., et al.: COVID-19 contact tracing: challenges and future directions. IEEE Access **8**, 225703–225729 (2020). https://doi.org/10.1109/ACCESS.2020.3036718

4. España, G., et al.: Impacts of k-12 school reopening on the COVID-19 epidemic in Indiana USA. Epidemics **37**, 100487 (2020). https://doi.org/10.1101/2020.08.22.20179960

5. Espinoza, B., et al.: Asymptomatic individuals can increase the final epidemic size under adaptive human behavior. Sci. Rep. **11**(1), 1–12 (2021). https://doi.org/10.1038/s41598-021-98999-2

6. European Centre for Disease Prevention and Control: Assessment of the further emergence and potential impact of the SARS-CoV-2 Omicron variant of concern in the context of ongoing transmission of the Delta variant of concern in the EU/EEA, 18th update (2021). www.ecdc.europa.eu/en/publications-data/covid-19-assessment-further-emergence-omicron-18th-risk-assessment

7. Ghorbani, A., et al.: The ASSOCC simulation model: A response to the community call for the COVID-19 pandemic. Rev. Artif. Soc. Soc. Simul. (2020). https://rofasss.org/2020/04/25/the-assocc-simulation-model/

8. Google: COVID-19 Community Mobility Reports. www.google.com/covid19/mobility/index.html. Accessed 28 01 2022

9. Hall, V.J., et al.: SARS-CoV-2 infection rates of antibody-positive compared with antibody-negative health-care workers in England: a large, multicentre, prospective cohort study (SIREN). Lancet **397**(10283), 1459–1469 (2021). https://doi.org/10.1016/S0140-6736(21)00675-9

10. Lee, J.: Mental health effects of school closures during COVID-19. Lancet Child Adolesc. Health **4**(6), 421 (2020). https://doi.org/10.1016/S2352-4642(20)30109-7

11. Lorig, F., et al.: Agent-based social simulation of the COVID-19 pandemic: a systematic review. J. Artif. Soc. Soc. Simul. **24**(3), 5 (2021). https://doi.org/10.18564/jasss.4601

12. Mossong, J., et al.: Social contacts and mixing patterns relevant to the spread of infectious diseases. PLoS Med. **5**(3), 0381–0391 (2008). https://doi.org/10.1371/journal.pmed.0050074

13. Phillips, B., et al.: Model-based projections for COVID-19 outbreak size and student-days lost to closure in Ontario childcare centers and primary schools. Sci. Rep. **11**(1), 1–14 (2020). https://doi.org/10.1101/2020.08.07.20170407

14. Robert Koch-Institut: SARS-CoV-2 Infektionen in Deutschland (2022). https://doi.org/10.5281/zenodo.5908707

15. Schuler, C.F., IV., et al.: Mild SARS-CoV-2 illness is not associated with reinfections and provides persistent spike, nucleocapsid, and virus-neutralizing antibodies. Microbio. Spectr. **9**(2), e00087–21 (2021). https://doi.org/10.1128/Spectrum.00087-21

16. Shinde, G.R., Kalamkar, A.B., Mahalle, P.N., Dey, N., Chaki, J., Hassanien, A.E.: Forecasting models for coronavirus disease (COVID-19): a survey of the state-of-the-art. SN Comput. Sci. **1**(4), 1–15 (2020). https://doi.org/10.1007/s42979-020-00209-9

17. Squazzoni, F., et al.: Computational models that matter during a global pandemic outbreak: a call to action. J. Artif. Soc. Soc. Simul. **23**(2), 10 (2020). https://doi.org/10.18564/jasss.4298

18. Timm, I.J., et al.: Kognitive Sozialsimulation für das COVID-19-Krisenmanagement - Social Simulation for Analysis of Infectious Disease Control (SoSAD). Technical report Deutsches Forschungszentrum für Künstliche Intelligenz (DFKI) (2020)

Generating Explanatory Saliency Maps for Mixed Traffic Flow Using a Behaviour Cloning Model

Yasin M. Yousif(✉) and Jörg P. Müller

Department of Informatics, Clausthal University of Technology,
Clausthal-Zellerfeld, Germany
{yasin.yousif,joerg.mueller}@tu-clausthal.de

Abstract. Multi-agent mixed traffic modelling and simulation are needed for safety estimation of traffic situations. Many of the most accurate traffic prediction models use deep learning methods that are considered black box models. This means that the output cannot be directly interpreted based on the input. However, such interpretation can be valuable in providing explanatory information about the model predictions for a simulation or a real-world dataset.

On the other hand, formulating the prediction problem as states to actions mapping problem namely in a markov decision process (MDP) framework is a more realistic approach to fully imitate the traffic entity behaviour. Therefore, a behaviour cloning approach with memoryless architecture is presented here. As a result, it is easier to link the output to the image input using saliency maps extraction methods.

The saliency maps calculated from the trained model highlight the traversable areas for the agent to reach its destination, avoiding collision with other agents and obstacles. They also show the salient roads edges that influence the direction of the predicted movement. These results are based on an analysis of a representative set of examples from the dataset.

Keywords: Mixed traffic modelling · Behaviour cloning · Saliency maps

1 Introduction

Traffic simulation is needed for estimation, optimization, prediction and understanding of vehicular or pedestrian traffic [1]. For example, it can help city planners evaluate the safety level in any proposed urban structure. However, the case of mixed traffic is more challenging than single mode traffic due to the higher complexity in the interactions between the different modes (e.g. vehicles, pedestrians, or cyclists).

Many deep learning models for mixed traffic prediction was proposed in the literature [2–5]. Although they provide low errors for many traffic datasets [6–8],

© The Author(s), under exclusive license to Springer Nature Switzerland AG 2023
F. Lorig and E. Norling (Eds.): MABS 2022, LNAI 13743, pp. 107–120, 2023.
https://doi.org/10.1007/978-3-031-22947-3_9

they still lack a direct and accurate way to provide explanations of their predictions. This is due to the complexity and the size of their network architecture, which make the task of interpreting the output more difficult.

These interpretations are needed in traffic simulation programs because the output is only the trajectories of the different agents in the traffic area (The agent represents here the traffic entity model used in the simulation).

For example in Fig. 1, if the simulation shows that a pedestrian is slowing down at the edge of a road while a car is passing by, then there's no way to tell if the pedestrian is waiting for the car (case A) or if he is just turning around an obstacle on the sidewalk (case B). To make sure of the reason, one method is determining the most influencing item by the means of a heatmap generation for the input image.

These heatmaps that correspond to an input image of a neural network model are called saliency maps and the methods to calculate them belong to the category of pixels attributions methods [9]

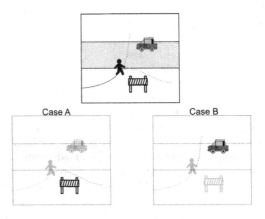

Fig. 1. Why the model is predicting a slowing and turning movement for the pedestrian?

The need for generating interpretations is also present in another field, namely, self-driving cars [10]. One important use case is to explain the software logic which led to an accident. It is also noted that traffic prediction modules are used as part of the self-driving cars software [11], therefore the same need for interpretation is present for these modules. However, the topic of interpretation in traffic prediction [12] did not receive as much attention as in the case of self-driving cars [13,14].

An important point to consider when designing the traffic agent model is matching the model's input and output with the real input and output of the traffic participant. Therefore, a model is proposed here where the output (the action) is determined using only the current input (the state), thus fulfilling the Markov property. The expected result is getting clear and meaningful saliency maps.

These maps are grayscale images highlighting the highest influencing regions of the input, which contributed towards the prediction. Although, this isn't a full interpretation, it still provides insights into the model internal reasoning process.

After training this model on the mixed traffic datasets, the evaluation is done with respect to the accuracy of its predictions, and by analysing a representative set of examples and showing its corresponding saliency maps.

The paper contribution is in proposing a model architecture capable of predicting realistic waypoints for the traffic entity and at the same time generating saliency maps with insights into the model internal reasoning.

In the next section, a review of deep learning traffic models and visual explanation methods is presented. After that, a perspective on a multi-agent implementation of the model is discussed. Section 3 presents the neural network architecture, as well as the implemented saliency map extraction method. The results in quantitative way, and a set of saliency maps are shown in Sect. 4. These results are discussed and general remarks are made in Sect. 5. Finally, Sect. 6 concludes this paper with an overview of the contribution.

2 Related Work

In the following, a review of a number of important previous work in the field of mixed traffic prediction, followed by a review of the most suitable saliency map extraction methods are presented. Finally, a multi-agent prospective of implementing this model is discussed.

2.1 Mixed Traffic Prediction Methods

In the topic of mixed traffic models, there are numerous methods available. Some depend on rule-based methods [1,15], while others use black box deep learning models [2,3,5]. The latter category showed lower errors for prediction in many traffic datasets [6–8]. However, this accuracy came at the cost of a more complex structure, bigger size of networks, and eventually lower explainability.

One of the first deep learning models with good accuracy is Social-LSTM [2]. This method uses a social pooling layer where the hidden vectors of different Long Short-Term Memory (LSTM) networks (each one correspond to a nearby traffic participant) is taken to predict the agent future trajectory.

Other later work [3] employed Generative Adversarial Network (GAN) architectures. It depended on random sampling to generate multiple plausible trajectories. Variational Auto-encoders Architecture (VAE) was used as well [16] where a random sampling step is also performed. However, in these two cases (GAN and VAE) the output is dependent on random factor which cannot be explained.

Recently the work in [17], used Inverse Reinforcement Learning network as a first part to predict the coarse goal and trajectory, and then other recurrent networks with attention layers were used to get the finer trajectory.

In order to implement a deep learning model for mixed traffic modelling and simulation with less complexity and with memoryless architecture, a direct architecture of successive Convolutional Neural Network (CNN) layers is adopted here. This will make the generated saliency maps more meaningful and understandable, otherwise, if an architecture with LSTM (which contains a memory) or with GAN (where a random sampling step is done) is used, the saliency maps will be affected by other random or previous input values, not just the current agent input.

Some additional previous methods did use similar architecture of successive CNN layers. One example is [18], where the input is a group of RGB images and the output is flattened to form a group of vectors representing multiple plausible paths. Another paper is Y-Net [5], where a U-Net architecture is used to predict the pedestrians trajectories and goals, with an input consisting of the scene image and the previous trajectory of the agent. However, the work here has a different shape of actions and states, targeted to make the process of generating the output more transparent.

2.2   Saliency Maps Extraction Methods

For the network architecture proposed here, a number of suitable methods for saliency maps extraction are reviewed in the following.

Attention maps [19] are heatmaps generated using an additional layer added at the beginning of the network, and trained with it. This layer is multiplied with its input, in inference time, in order to maximize the effect of the important areas while minimizing the effect of other areas in the input.

The Visual Backprop [14] method depends on the usage of the most influencing information found in the higher layers, then by alternating between a deconvolution operation and element-wise multiplication with the activation matrix of the previous layer, moving from the output towards the input, it can link the output with the input as shown in Fig. 2, taken from [14]. The end result is a grayscale image where the most salient parts of the input are highlighted.

Recently the work in [13], called attentional bottleneck, proposes the usage of an attention layer while fusing the input into a smaller layer where the data is forced into smaller size making the heatmap more focused on the most salient parts of the input.

All of the previous methods can generate visual explanations in the form of heatmaps. In this work, the method of visual backprob is selected to generate the maps, due to its suitability to the architecture. For instance, it was implemented with the similar architecture of PilotNet [20].

In the field of traffic prediction, previous attempts to generate visual explanations were done. One example, is the paper in [4] where an attention layer is used to get saliency maps. The result highlighted the traversability parts of the scene. Another work [12] used a Layer-wise Relevance Propagation (LRP) [21] method to assign a percentage to each agent in the scene representing its influence on the prediction output. These two methods reported some benefits of applying post-hoc explanation methods to the traffic prediction models.

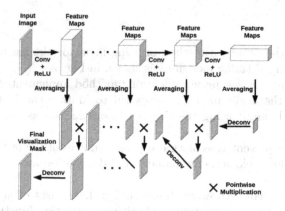

Fig. 2. VisualBackProp explanation method workflow (taken from [14] page 4703)

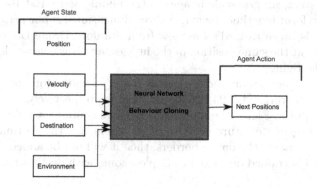

Fig. 3. Overview of the behaviour cloning approach for traffic modelling

2.3   Multi-agent Perspective of Mixed Traffic Modelling

The problem of mixed traffic modelling is a multi-agent problem by nature, where different types of agents should be represented by different types of models. Additionally, each model should be customizable in order to represent the different agent attributes on microscopic level.

In this work, the goal is to mimic the single agent behavior, by presenting the problem as states to actions mapping. All the traffic types (pedestrians, cyclists and cars) are using the same model with a multi-heads output architecture, as shown in Fig. 4, so each output branch can become specialized in a particular traffic type. However, to represent the complex interaction space between different agents additional modelling of theses interaction are needed. The interactions include behaviours like collaboration or communication among agents. Therefore the current model can be used to represent the single agent logic and then be integrated with other models to represent the interactions separately.

3   Method

An overview of the proposed method of using behavior cloning in the problem of microscopic mixed traffic modelling is shown in Fig. 3

Behavior cloning is a supervised learning method implemented within MDP settings, where the agent model is supposed to imitate the behaviour of the expert (usually human) using the expert demonstrations as the training data [22].

The state is represented as several top-view images of the last eight steps of the agent. Position, velocity, environment and destination are encoded in those images.

The network architecture, as shown in Fig. 4, consists of successive CNN layers with relu activation functions and softmax activation function for the last layer. The input is several RGB and grayscale images, specifically, one RGB image at the start, six grayscale images in the middle and a last RGB image at the end. They form together the single three dimensional input array.

The input is taken as bird's eye view from Stanford Drone Dataset [6]. The agent is always at the same position in the images, and it is color-coded as shown in Fig. 5 at the right.

The standard prediction and trajectory history lengths for this dataset are, as in many other works [4,5,23], 3600 and 2400 ms respectively.

As shown also in Fig. 4, the input step 8 image contains a yellow dot representing an approximate future position of the agent, i.e. the destination. If the destination fell outside the image borders, then it will not be added. This means that the model is trained on mixed examples, some with destination and others without.

The output contains twelve grayscale images, representing the agent probability of being in a given position for the respective twelve steps. This is similar to the output format used in [11]. In other words, the (x,y) coordinate of the predicted future position is encoded in 2D array as a peak value of a probability distribution.

The nature of the trajectory prediction problem is not deterministic [5]. This means that there isn't one possible correct prediction but many plausible outputs. To represent this feature, different works used different approaches, for example by using generative architecture [3], variational auto-encoders [16], or multi head architecture [18].

In this work a multi-head output is implemented, as shown in Fig. 4. The exact number of output paths for Stanford Drone Dataset is either 20 or 5 based on the standard split used in other works [23].

After the training phase, the predictions are calculated from the model on the test split of the dataset. Simultaneously the explanatory saliency maps are generated for each output using the visual backprop method.

Small modifications are done here on top of visual backprop method. Namely, for each activation layer and before performing the multiplication operation, the layer's values are normalized to the range (0–1), and a histogram equalization step is performed on the last heatmap that corresponds to the input.

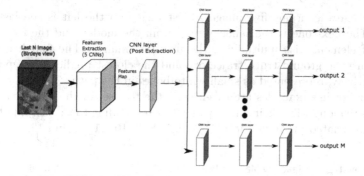

Fig. 4. Network architecture

4   Experimental Evaluation

The result of training the network for single, 5 and 20 modes on Stanford Dataset is shown in Table 1 where the errors are in pixels, namely the Average Displacement Error (ADE), and Final Displacement Error (FDE).

The mode is the term used in many other papers [17,18,24] to indicate the number of plausible paths in the model output generated for a single agent state, i.e. multi-modal model.

Table 1. The errors in pixels for different numbers of modes on the Stanford Drone Dataset along with the result of other papers

Case	ADE (pixel)	FDE (pixel)	Epochs of training
BC[a] - 1 mode	30	450	111
BC - 5 modes	21.99	211.78	30
BC - 20 modes	17.99	273.9	36
BC - 20 modes (no destination)	29.47	317.25	36
Social GAN[b] [3] (20 modes)	27.23	41.44	–
CF-VAE [16] (20 modes)	12.60	22.30	–
Y-Net[b] [5] (20 modes)	7.85	11.85	–

[a] Behaviour Cloning (Ours)
[b] It predicts only pedestrians movement

The saliency maps examples were chosen according to two criteria, in order to be a representative set of examples. First criterion, the ADE should be lower than twelve pixels for all the examples. Second criterion, these examples should be crowded, and diverse with respect to the agents' types. s The real and synthetic examples are shown in Figs. (5 to 16), where the black path represents the ground truth, the pink paths represent the predictions, and the blue path represent the past trajectory.

Each figure contains five images. First image on the left is the last input image. The next one is the saliency map from the model, and the third is the result of element-wise multiplying the first two images. The fourth and fifth images are the ground truth trajectory and the closest predicted waypoints to it respectively, represented as small white boxes in the path.

The following examples are taken from the test set of the dataset and presented here along with their saliency maps corresponding to the last input image and its associated prediction in Figs. 5, 6, 7, 8, 9, 10, 11, 12 and 13.

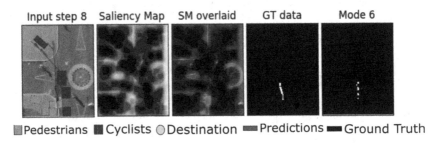

Fig. 5. Scenario 1 – 20 modes output

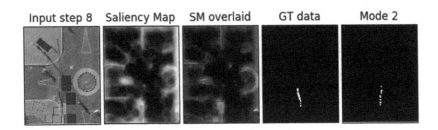

Fig. 6. Scenario 1 – 5 modes output

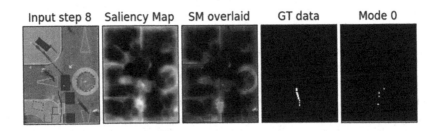

Fig. 7. Scenario 1 – single mode output

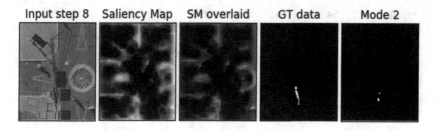

Fig. 8. Scenario 1 – 20 modes output without destination

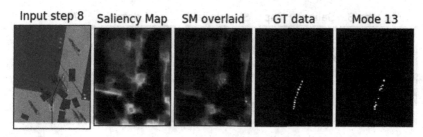

Fig. 9. Scenario 2 – 20 modes output

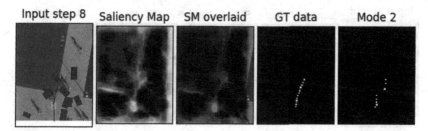

Fig. 10. Scenario 2 – 5 modes output

Figures 5, 6, 7, 8 belong to the same traffic scenario, but with output for networks of 20, 5 and single modes as well as 20 modes without destination, respectively. The most accurate output is for the 20 modes with destination as shown in Fig. 5, where the cyclists are avoided and blackened out in the saliency maps, but a path very close to the ground truth is taken.

The five-modes network predicted a path near the ground truth also, as shown in Fig. 6 and the same is true for the one-mode output. Without destination, the network also excludes the area next to the cyclists.

In Figs. 9 and 10, the pedestrian wants to cross between two cyclists. The saliency maps shows a thin line between the pedestrian and the destination in both of the two networks. However, in both of them there is a jump in the best output prediction which is clearly due to the closeness of the passing-by cyclists.

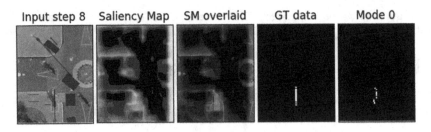

Fig. 11. Scenario 3 – 20 modes output

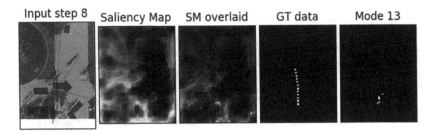

Fig. 12. Scenario 4 – 20 modes output

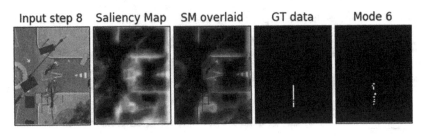

Fig. 13. Scenario 5 – 20 modes without destination

Figures 11 and 12 are for two separate examples. Here it is clear also that not only the nearby cyclists' and pedestrians' rectangles are blackened out, but also the road in front of them where they may pass in the future.

Figure 13 shows that even without destination the output is in the direction of the ground truth, and as the saliency maps shows, big black areas are in the way because of the cyclists.

Figure 14 is a synthetic example, where three pedestrians try to cross the road and a fast car has just passed them. The prediction is a jump to the sidewalk, and a few points suggest a movement to the left towards the destination. Here the sidewalk is highlighted along with the car and the pedestrians rectangles. Figure 15 also shows a focus on the sidewalk as well as further movement in the direction of the sidewalk. Figure 16, the model correctly avoided the cyclists and tried to take a turning behind the obstacle to the destination. The agent, the obstacle and the destination are all highlighted.

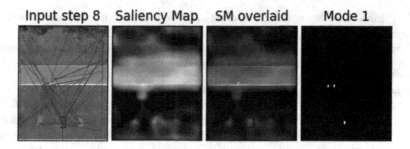

Fig. 14. Scenario 6 - synthetic example 20 modes

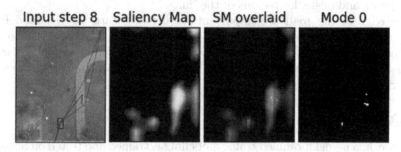

Fig. 15. Scenario 7 - synthetic example 5 modes

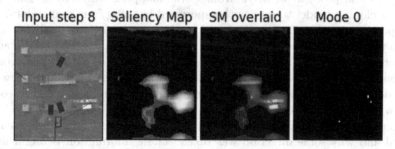

Fig. 16. Scenario 8 - synthetic example single mode

5 Discussion

The error values were slightly higher for the model here than some other methods shown in Table 1, even with destination. However, the errors are considered reasonable given that the state image dimensions are 640 × 480, so an ADE of 20–30 pixels is around 3–5% error in height and 4–6% error in width. Additionally, the extraction of meaningful saliency maps is possible with this level of accuracy.

The network does the prediction by detecting patterns of agents positions and environment structure in the input images. These patterns should be highlighted in the saliency maps, and by analyzing these maps it is noted that:

- They highlight the agent of interest, the yellow dot of destination and the edges of the road and sidewalks
- They blacken out the other faster agents in the vicinity of the main agent and the area in their movement direction.

In general, it is easy for the network to detect the agent, because of its basic color and position. It is also easy to detect the yellow destination point. The next step for the network is finding the correct path towards the destination. If the road is clear, it will be a straight path and it will be highlighted in the map. However, if other agents, like in Fig. 9, or some obstacles like in Fig. 16, were in the way, then a maneuver should be done, and the saliency map will blacken out these agents and obstacles regions of the image.

The edge of the road are important features to learn for the model, for example in Fig. 9, the edge is tilted, the prediction path is also parallel to that one, because it's more likely to walk in the direction of (or perpendicular to) the road direction than in other ways. This is also shown in Fig. 5, when the pedestrian wants to cross the road.

6   Conclusion

In this work, a model for mixed traffic modelling is trained and tested on Stanford Drone Dataset for three agent types (cars, cyclists and pedestrians). This model formulates the problem in MDP framework, mapping states to actions using behavior cloning model trained with supervised learning from traffic data.

A post-hoc explanation method was used to get explanatory saliency maps for the predictions. These maps showed that the model attended to the agent, the destination and the possible areas to plan the predicted path, while avoiding collision with other agents and obstacles. The edges of the roads and sidewalks, which define the general direction of movement were also highlighted in consistency with the predictions.

Therefore, these maps can provide more information of why some area was avoided and why some direction was taken. These information is useful in the case of a simulation or in the case of automatic analysis of real-world dataset.

As a future work, a method for assigning each output branch of the model to specific traffic participant type should be investigated in order to use the model to drive different agents in a multi-agent based simulation framework.

Another future direction is analysing the saliency maps for continuous movement of the agent model and for interaction scenarios from the perspective of the different interacting agents.

Acknowledgement. This work was supported by the German Academic Exchange Service (DAAD) under the Graduate School Scholarship Programme (GSSP).

References

1. Schönauer, R.: A microscopic traffic flow model for shared space. Graz University of Technology (2017)

2. Alahi, A., Goel, K., Ramanathan, V., Robicquet, A., Fei-Fei, L., Savarese, S.: Social lstm: human trajectory prediction in crowded spaces. In: Proceedings of the IEEE Conference on Computer Vision and Pattern Recognition, pp. 961–971 (2016)
3. Gupta, A., Johnson, J., Fei-Fei, L., Savarese, S., Alahi, A.: Social gan: socially acceptable trajectories with generative adversarial networks. In: Proceedings of the IEEE Conference on Computer Vision and Pattern Recognition, pp. 2255–2264 (2018)
4. Sadeghian, A., Kosaraju, V., Sadeghian, A., Hirose, N., Rezatofighi, H., Savarese, S.: Sophie: an attentive gan for predicting paths compliant to social and physical constraints. In: Proceedings of the IEEE/CVF Conference on Computer Vision and Pattern Recognition, pp. 1349–1358 (2019)
5. Mangalam, K., An, Y., Girase, H., Malik, J.: From goals, waypoints & paths to long term human trajectory forecasting. In: Proceedings of the IEEE/CVF International Conference on Computer Vision, pp. 15233–15242 (2021)
6. Robicquet, A., Sadeghian, A., Alahi, A., Savarese, S.: Learning social etiquette: human trajectory understanding in crowded scenes. In: Leibe, B., Matas, J., Sebe, N., Welling, M. (eds.) ECCV 2016. LNCS, vol. 9912, pp. 549–565. Springer, Cham (2016). https://doi.org/10.1007/978-3-319-46484-8_33
7. Bock, J., Krajewski, R., Moers, T., Runde, S., Vater, L., Eckstein, L.: The ind dataset: a drone dataset of naturalistic road user trajectories at German intersections. In: 2020 IEEE Intelligent Vehicles Symposium (IV), pp. 1929–1934 (2020)
8. Caesar, H., et al.: nuscenes: a multimodal dataset for autonomous driving. In: CVPR (2020)
9. Molnar, C.: Interpretable Machine Learning. Lulu.com (2020)
10. Zablocki, É., Ben-Younes, H., Pérez, P., Cord, M.: Explainability of vision-based autonomous driving systems: review and challenges. arXiv preprint. arXiv:2101.05307 (2021)
11. Bansal, M., Krizhevsky, A., Ogale, A.: Chauffeurnet: learning to drive by imitating the best and synthesizing the worst. arXiv preprint. arXiv:1812.03079 (2018)
12. Kothari, P., Kreiss, S., Alahi, A.: Human trajectory forecasting in crowds: a deep learning perspective. IEEE Trans. Intell. Transp. Syst. **23**, 7386–7400 (2021)
13. Kim, J., Bansal, M.: Attentional bottleneck: towards an interpretable deep driving network. In: Proceedings of the IEEE/CVF Conference on Computer Vision and Pattern Recognition Workshops, pp. 322–323 (2020)
14. Bojarski, M., et al.: Visualbackprop: efficient visualization of cnns for autonomous driving. In: 2018 IEEE International Conference on Robotics and Automation (ICRA). IEEE, pp. 4701–4708 (2018)
15. Johora, F.T., Müller, J.P.: Modeling interactions of multimodal road users in shared spaces. In: 2018 21st International Conference on Intelligent Transportation Systems (ITSC), IEEE (2018) 3568–3574
16. Bhattacharyya, A., Hanselmann, M., Fritz, M., Schiele, B., Straehle, C.N.: Conditional flow variational autoencoders for structured sequence prediction. arXiv preprint. arXiv:1908.09008 (2019)
17. Deo, N., Trivedi, M.M.: Trajectory forecasts in unknown environments conditioned on grid-based plans. arXiv preprint. arXiv:2001.00735 (2020)
18. Cui, H., et al.: Multimodal trajectory predictions for autonomous driving using deep convolutional networks. In: 2019 International Conference on Robotics and Automation (ICRA). IEEE, pp. 2090–2096 (2019)
19. Xu, K., et al.: Show, attend and tell: neural image caption generation with visual attention. In: International Conference on Machine Learning. PMLR, pp. 2048–2057 (2015)

20. Bojarski, M., et al.: Explaining how a deep neural network trained with end-to-end learning steers a car. arXiv preprint. arXiv:1704.07911 (2017)
21. Bach, S., Binder, A., Montavon, G., Klauschen, F., Müller, K.R., Samek, W.: On pixel-wise explanations for non-linear classifier decisions by layer-wise relevance propagation. PLoS ONE **10**(7), e0130140 (2015)
22. Osa, T., Pajarinen, J., Neumann, G., Bagnell, J.A., Abbeel, P., Peters, J.: An algorithmic perspective on imitation learning. arXiv preprint. arXiv:1811.06711 (2018)
23. Sadeghian, A., Kosaraju, V., Gupta, A., Savarese, S., Alahi, A.: Trajnet: towards a benchmark for human trajectory prediction. arXiv preprint (2018)
24. Mangalam, K., et al.: It is not the journey but the destination: endpoint conditioned trajectory prediction. In: Vedaldi, A., Bischof, H., Brox, T., Frahm, J.-M. (eds.) ECCV 2020. LNCS, vol. 12347, pp. 759–776. Springer, Cham (2020). https://doi.org/10.1007/978-3-030-58536-5_45

Challenges for Multi-Agent Based Agricultural Workforce Management

Helen Harman[✉][iD] and Elizabeth I. Sklar[iD]

Lincoln Institute for Agri-food Technology, University of Lincoln, Lincoln, UK
{hharman,esklar}@lincoln.ac.uk

Abstract. Multi-agent task allocation methods seek to distribute a set of tasks fairly amongst a set of agents. In real-world settings, such as soft fruit farms, human labourers undertake harvesting tasks, assigned by farm managers. The work here explores the application of artificial intelligence planning methodologies to optimise the existing workforce and applies multi-agent based simulation to evaluate the efficacy of the AI strategies. Key challenges threatening the acceptance of such an approach are highlighted and solutions are evaluated experimentally.

Keywords: Agriculture · Multi-agent based simulation · Task allocation

1 Introduction

On farms that grow high-value crops, such as soft fruit (e.g. strawberries, raspberries, cherries), field vegetables (e.g. broccoli, cauliflower) and ornamentals (e.g. daffodils), seasonal workers are hired to pick ripe produce at harvest time. Shortages in seasonal labour, due to a variety of global political, social, economic and health factors [4,13,19] are motivating farmers to seek innovative solutions for managing their harvest workforce—otherwise, farms may be left with plants unharvested, which is both costly and wasteful [20]. To help address this situation, we have been exploring the application of *artificial intelligence (AI)* planning methodologies to optimise the existing workforce and *multi-agent based simulation (MABS)* to evaluate the efficacy of our strategies. Although our methods and simulation results are backed by real-world data sourced from a commercial farm, there are a number of key challenges that we have faced along the way that could threaten the acceptance of such an approach. Here we describe these challenges and present our solutions designed to mitigate their impact.

The first challenge is centred around how to handle the different types of incrementally produced data so that our solution can be deployed when it is needed. In general, there are two types of data that we can obtain from farms: *historic* data, which records what happened in the past; and *prognostic* data, which estimates what will happen in the future. Most modern farms maintain detailed historic electronic records describing the resources expended and labour

F. Lorig and E. Norling (Eds.): MABS 2022, LNAI 13743, pp. 121–133, 2023.
https://doi.org/10.1007/978-3-031-22947-3_10

activities. This helps farm managers to minimise costs in a sector that traditionally operates at very low margins and with high risk due to dependence on unpredictable factors such as the weather and the availability of appropriately skilled farm labour. In order to plan ahead—on a daily basis as well as seasonally—farmers also develop detailed estimates describing when crops should be planted, tended and harvested. This includes associated volumes and locations, as well as the size and skills of the labour force required to accomplish the planting, crop care and harvesting tasks.

The second challenge relates to the application of multi-agent based simulation to assess the impact of our proposed AI planning strategies for managing the workforce as compared to the baseline, the manual strategies currently employed on farms. Typically, this involves farm managers wrangling spreadsheets in order to determine who is available on any given day to perform the range of tasks that must be completed. While farms do record many aspects of harvesting, they do not record details that would better inform a more accurate simulation of workforce, such as tracking where individuals walk in fields and when they take breaks. Although it is technically possible to record such data, this is not something that workers are happy about—being watched by "big brother" is uncomfortable, especially for many migrant workers, and could cause workers to quit their jobs and seek work on other farms where they are not being watched so closely. So we are challenged by wanting to show improvement within a simulation that is not a completely accurate portrayal of what is happening in the real world.

The third challenge is the workforce management strategy itself. In earlier work [6,7], we explored different methods of assigning workers to fields and tasks to workers in the fields. Here we challenge some of the assumptions we have made in that work, particularly around modelling workers for whom we have no historic data.

This paper is organised as follows. Section 2 provides background on the specific fruit farm use case we simulate here and briefly discusses AI and multi-agent applications in agriculture. Section 3 describes the approach we have developed to address the challenges mentioned above. Sections 4 and 5 present our experiments and results. Section 6 summarises our work and highlights next steps.

2   Background

On soft fruit farms, each day during harvest season a farm manager determines which fields are ready for picking and how many groups of workers, or "teams", are needed. Each team harvests one or more fields; the manager decides which workers to assign to each team and which team to assign to each field. When fruit pickers arrive at the fields, team leaders assign picking areas for each worker. Pickers harvest ripe fruits and place them in containers held in trays; filled trays are then transported to packing stations where they are weighed and tallied to record the volume picked and by whom— often pickers are remunerated based on the volume of ripe fruits they pick. This picking information provides a rich data set from which a range of different models could be derived, including the multi-agent model developed here.

Potential opportunities for multi-agent and multi-robot methodologies applied within the agriculture domain are analysed and characterised in [16]. This includes use of autonomous robots to drive in fields and collect sensor data [4], which is analysed using machine vision methods to identify ripe fruit [11], map regions in need of irrigation [1], or locate weeds [15], as well as robotic solutions for picking and transporting crops [5,14,24]. Some researchers have experimentally evaluated hybrid human-robot solutions, where robots transport produce while humans do the picking [2,23]. In our previous work [7], we showed how *Multi-Robot Task Allocation (MRTA)* strategies—evaluated using our simulator (see Sect. 3.3)—can be used to suggest the best ratio of "runners" (workers who transport produce) to pickers.

MRTA problems address situations in which a group of robots must work together to complete a set of tasks. A popular family of solutions to MRTA problems are market-based *auction mechanisms*. As described in the literature [3, 9,10], auctions are executed in *rounds* that are typically composed of three phases: (i) announce tasks—an *auction manager* advertises one or more tasks to the agents; (ii) compute bids—each agent determines its individual valuation (cost or utility) for one or more of the announced tasks and offers a *bid* for any relevant tasks; and (iii) determine winner—the auction manager decides which agent(s) are awarded which task(s).

There is a substantial body of work on the application of auction-based mechanisms to the problem of allocating tasks for multi-agent teams. A popular method within the literature is the *sequential single-item (SSI)* method [12]. In SSI, all unassigned tasks are announced to the bidders and the bidder that responses with the best (e.g. shortest duration) bid for any task is allocated that task. The auction repeats in rounds until all tasks have been allocated. Auction mechanisms take into account both the self-interests of individual bidders as well as group goal(s) represented by the auction manager. Various variations on SSI have been proposed. Heap & Pagnucco [8] proposed *sequential single-cluster (SSC)* auctions for solving pick-up and delivery tasks in a dynamic environment. SSC announces and assigns *clusters* of geographically neighbouring tasks in each round, instead of only assigning one task (SSI).

Schneider et al. [22] conducted an empirical analysis of different auction-based mechanisms: SSI, *ordered single-item (OSI)*, *parallel single-item (PSI)* and *round robin (RR)* (as the simple baseline). Results revealed that the advantages of SSI can be greatly diminished when tasks are dynamically allocated over time. Subsequently, the performance of task allocation mechanisms in a set of parameterised mission environments was investigated [21]. Results showed that some task allocation methods consistently outperformed all others—but only under specific mission parameters. In the environments evaluated, no single method managed to outperform all others across all sets of parameters.

In our early attempts to address to the problem of assigning workers to fields (as outlined in Sect. 3.2), we compared SSI with RR. Although an in-depth investigation and comparison is planned in future work, our preliminary results showed more favourable performance with RR. Thus the approach presented here is based on RR. RR benefits from low computation costs and results in (roughly) even distribution of tasks (i.e. the number of tasks each agent is assigned differs at most by 1 when any agent is capable of performing any of the tasks on offer). For MRTA problems, RR alone can result in inefficient task allocations. We therefore modify the output of RR to improve the solution's efficiency.

3   Approach

This section describes our overall approach in which we applied multi-agent based simulation to compare different methods of managing human labour on a soft fruit farm. First, we model the behaviour of individual workers. Second, we group workers into teams. Third we use a simulator to evaluate the teams.

3.1   Modelling Workers

We model human workers—fruit pickers—using a data-backed model, built on information that is already collected on many farms, as explained below. This "worker model" is based on an estimate of how quickly a picker harvests each type of fruit grown on the farm. Different types of fruit require different techniques for harvesting and thus different skills. For each type of fruit, each picker is assigned a different *picking speed*, in grams per second, computed for each type of fruit they have picked previously[1]. This is calculated by dividing the amount of fruit a picker picked by the duration the picker picked for, and finding the average over all dates they picked that type of fruit.

If we encounter a worker who has not picked a certain type of fruit (i.e. does not have any historic information in our data set), we cannot assume that the worker is not able to pick that fruit. They could be a new worker whose experience is unknown to our system, or could be a worker who has never previously been assigned to a field with a particular type of fruit. To set the speed of these workers we cluster the pickers, using *k-means clustering* [18], and use the center of the cluster as the speed of all pickers in that cluster. When the clusters are sorted, this enables us to determine a rank (in $[0\ldots(k-1)]$) for each worker (for each type of fruit they have picked). Our experiments look at the effect that using a different default rank and clustering has on our results (see Sect. 5).

3.2   Team Creation

Our team creation method involves two steps: (i) creating an initial solution using Round-Robin; and (ii) improving the solution to minimise the variance in

---

[1] Note that at least two trays of the same type of fruit must be recorded in order to calculate a picking speed for that fruit. If there are not at least two trays recorded in the data set, then the picker is assigned the default picking speed—like workers who have not picked any fruit of that type.

the estimated field picking times across all fields. An overview of our method (and variations) has been presented in an extended abstract [6].

The first step in our method is to generate an initial solution, using RR. Workers are sorted slowest first, using their average picking speed over all fruits. Fields are sorted by yield (lowest first). RR assigns the first worker to the first field, the second worker to the second field and so forth. After a single worker has been assigned to each field, the fields are re-iterated over to assign each of them a second worker, and so forth until all workers have been allocated.

The second step in our method improves the solution by reassigning workers from fields requiring less picking time to fields requiring more picking time. This involves first computing the estimated picking time (ept) for each field (f) for a particular date (d), assuming it is picked by a specific team of workers (W). This is calculated by dividing the *estimated yield* (for field f on date d) by the sum of the workers' picking speeds. After calculating the initial ept of each field, our approach creates a list of pairs of fields that is sorted by the difference in estimated picking time between the two fields (Δept). The pair of fields with the largest Δept appears first, and the rest are taken in descending order of Δept. Then the algorithm searches for the picker who, when moved from the field with the shortest picking time to the field with the longest picking time (in each pair of fields), produces a reduced Δept. We call this the "candidate worker". If no worker is moved (i.e. because moving a worker would increase Δept or the field with the shortest duration has two or fewer workers), then the pair of fields is removed from the list of all pairs of fields. The algorithm continues until the list of pairs of fields is empty.

3.3   Simulating Teams

We have constructed a *multi-agent based simulation* to evaluate our proposed teams and compare them to the actual teams manually created by farm managers. Our simulator was developed using MASON [17], a discrete-event multi-agent simulation library and was introduced in previous work [7], where it was used to evaluate different methods of allocating tasks to workers within each team. The work here expands on this by bundling and sorting picking tasks. In our simulator, picking tasks are represented by patches (areas) of fruits that are ripe, as illustrated in Fig. 1. The colour of the patches represents the number of ripe fruits: red patches contain more ripe fruits than orange, which contain more than yellow, and green indicates low amounts of ripe fruits.

An agent in our system is a fruit picker and is defined by the tuple $p = \langle v, \ell, s_p, c \rangle$, where ℓ is the agent's initial location, v its navigation speed and s_p its picking speed (grams per step). When a picker has reached their capacity (c), they transport the picked fruit to a packing station.

Tasks are allocated to pickers using SSI. A picking task is defined as an (x, y) location and a number of ripe fruits. The cost of a picking bid is the *duration* for the agent to complete all their previously assigned tasks plus the task being auctioned. The duration of a single picking task is the sum of three components: the time it takes the agent to navigate to their picking location; the time it takes

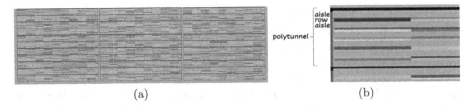

Fig. 1. Example of a commercial field: (a) within our simulator, and (b) a zoomed-in section highlighting areas within the polytunnel, namely a *row* where plants are growing, colour-coded according to ripeness, and *aisle*, the space between rows where pickers move. Each field has multiple horizontally and vertically adjacent polytunnels (the example field has 3 × 11 polytunnels) containing rows of crops, which are reached via aisles (the example polytunnels have 5 rows and 6 aisles). Each row contains two vertically adjacent fruit patches and can be any number of patches long (e.g. 10). See text for explanation of the colours. (Color figure online)

to pick the ripe fruits; and, when c is reached, the time it takes to navigate to the packing station, drop off the fruits (currently a fixed value set to one timestep) and return to the patch.

Rather than a picker bidding on a single task, tasks can be *bundled* together by row and which aisle the picking is executed in, i.e. the row is split in half lengthwise (for the example shown in Fig. 1, each bundle will contain 10 tasks). This will decrease the distance travelled by agents and the likelihood of agents obstructing each other (since an agent will travel between fewer rows). When bidding on a bundled task, an agent will create bids for each of the independent picking tasks in a bundle, and the cost for the bundle will be the cost of the picker executing all its previously assigned tasks plus the tasks in the bundle.

To further optimise a picker's independent schedule, their tasks are sorted by (x, y) location. The agent will pick the row with the lowest x position (starting at the lowest y position) and then pick the second to lowest row, and so forth. This sorting occurs during the bidding process. The timings of all tasks proceeding the one being bid on are (provisionally) updated, and the cost of the bid is set to the end time of the last task. If the agent wins the task, the provisional task timings are retained.

4   Experiments

We received data from a commercial fruit farm during the 2021 picking season, covering 182 picking days and 30 fields. Each field contained one of four types of soft fruit (strawberries, raspberries, blackberries or cherries). Our experiments assess our approach in the face of the three challenges introduced in Sect. 1:

1. Modelling from historic vs real-time and prognostic data:
   - *Historic:* The entire season of picking data was processed to create the worker model. Therefore, which worker is capable of picking each fruit is

known. The default picking rank is only used when the picker has picked too few fruits to be able to calculate their picking speed.

- *Live:* Only data recorded up to any given day is available, thus yield estimates are based on prognostic assessments by farm managers and worker models are based on picking records only up to the day before the one being planned. This is the data that would be available if our system were running on a farm and managing labour on a daily basis.

2. Simulating actual vs proposed teams:
- *Actual:* These are the results of using the teams created by farm managers (i.e. teams actually deployed), as produced by our simulator.
- *Proposed:* These are the results of using the teams proposed by our methods (described in Sect. 3), as produced by the same simulator.

3. Clustering and determining default rank picking speed:
- *Def_rank:* This is the default rank to use for modelling a worker when there is no information about that worker in the data set. Three values are compared: 3 (uses a mid-range picking speed), −1 (uses a picking speed lower than any worker with any experience) and * (uses the average picking speed over all workers).
- *N_clusters:* This is the number of clusters used for grouping workers. Two values are compared: 6 and $|W|$, where the latter is effectively "no clustering" since the number of clusters is equivalent to the number of workers. When the number of clusters is equal to $|W|$, the speed of the default rank is set to the average picking speed (denoted * above); otherwise the default rank is either 3 or −1.

Two metrics are recorded to evaluate the affect of the different conditions and parameter settings listed above. These are:

- **execution time:** The amount of simulator time for each picking date, for each field. In other words, the amount of time that elapses between when the team arrives at the field and when the team finishes picking that field. As some workers could spend less time working than others, particularly if the workload is unevenly distributed, we also calculate staff time.
- **staff time:** The sum of the simulator time worked by all workers each day, for each field. This metric is a proxy for payroll costs.

Experiments were executed to evaluate the performance of our workforce management strategy, specifically as it relates to the choices of grouping workers into clusters and assigning a picking speed for workers for whom we have no data: *(def_rank = 3, N_clusters = 6)* versus *(def_rank = −1, N_clusters = 6)* versus *(def_rank = *, N_clusters = |W|)*. Each experiment involved running our simulator under four conditions: *(Historic, Actual)*, *(Historic, Proposed)*, *(Live, Actual)* and *(Live, Proposed)*. For the *(Live, Proposed)* experiments, the estimated yield and list of available workers are used since the actual yield and worker list would not be available when a schedule were created. For the *Historic* and *(Live, Actual)* experiments, the actual list of workers and actual yield are used. There is no stochasticity, and thus, for each setup, the simulation is run once per date on each of the fields with a yield value.

5   Results

This section presents our experimental results. Numeric results are shown in Table 1. Plots are shown to compare the results; in all plots presented, error bars indicate ±1 standard deviation. All samples are normally distributed, as confirmed using the Shapiro-Wilk test for normality [25]. We compare the performance metrics for the *actual* teams and our *proposed* teams for each of the three parameter settings discussed previously. Tests for significance between *actual* and *proposed* teams are performed using Student's *t*-test for two independent samples. Tests for significance amongst the three parameter settings (*Def_rank* and *N_clusters* combinations) are performed using one-way analysis of variance (ANOVA) with three samples. For all statistical tests, we use $p < 0.01$.

Table 1. Experimental results showing *mean* (and *standard deviation*) of execution time and staff time for all variables and conditions evaluated. For *(Live, Proposed)*, the sample size is equal to the number of times the farm manager predicted a field would be picked. For the *Historic* and *(Live, Actual)*, the sample size is equal to the number of times a field was actually picked. Times are reported in terms of simulator time steps. The best values (shortest times) comparing parameters within one condition are highlighted in **bold**. The best values comparing between *actual* and *proposed* condition are highlighted in *italics*.

Conditions		Parameters		Sample	Resulting metrics	
Data	*Teams*	*Def_rank*	*N_clusters*	*Size*	*Execution time*	*Staff time*
Historic	Actual	3	6	1019	*23,265* (13,146)	577,402 (353,091)
Historic	Actual	−1	6	1019	*23,265* (13,146)	577,402 (353,091)
Historic	Actual	*	|W|	1019	**22,879** (12,905)	**551,283** (324,557)
Historic	Proposed	3	6	1019	**31,714** (10,423)	*522,211* (286,605)
Historic	Proposed	−1	6	1019	**31,714** (10,423)	*522,211* (286,605)
Historic	Proposed	*	|W|	1019	32,081 (12007)	**514,327** (279,039)
Live	Actual	3	6	1019	**23,594** (13,602)	**567,618** (340,717)
Live	Actual	−1	6	1019	*28,164* (23,912)	*621,310* (418,181)
Live	Actual	*	|W|	1019	24,817 (14,854)	580,586 (358,348)
Live	Proposed	3	6	1024	***19,303*** (7,179)	***430,891*** (207,562)
Live	Proposed	−1	6	1024	31,569 (12,942)	702,767 (394,499)
Live	Proposed	*	|W|	1024	*23,610* (7,765)	*536,844* (283,541)

5.1   Historic Data

First, we look at results obtained using the *historic* data set. When comparing the *actual* teams with our *proposed* teams, our proposed teams fare better for staff time than execution time. The actual teams produced a shorter *execution time* than our proposed teams; the difference is statistically significant for all three parameter settings (T-test scores for each pair, in the order listed in Table 1: $t = -16.07$, p = 0.000; $t = -16.07$, p = 0.0000; $t = -16.66$, p = 0.0000). However, our proposed teams resulted in a shorter *staff time* than the actual teams; again the difference is statistically significant for all three parameter settings (respectively: $t = 3.87$, p = 0.0001; $t = 3.87$, p = 0.0001; $t = 2.75$, p = 0.0060). **This is a positive result, since we are more concerned with reducing staff time than execution time.**

When comparing the three parameter settings, we find no statistically significant differences for either execution time (ANOVA scores for each triple within the Actual and Proposed times, respectively: F = 0.297, p = 0.7432; F = 0.378, p = 0.6852) or staff time (respectively: F = 1.958, p = 0.1413; F = 0.261, p = 0.7700). These are illustrated in Fig. 2.

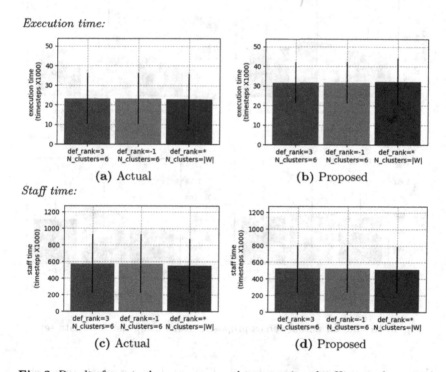

Fig. 2. Results for actual versus proposed teams using the *Historic* data set.

5.2   Live Data

Second, we look at results obtained using the *live* data set. When comparing the *actual* teams with our *proposed* teams, **our proposed teams have better**

results for both execution and staff time for two of the three parameter settings, excepting *(def_rank = -1, N_clusters = 6)*. The results for the
first two parameter settings for execution time are statistically significant, but
not for the third *(def_rank = *, N_clusters = |W|)* (*t*-test scores, in the order
listed in Table 1: t = 8.919, p = 0.0000; t = -4.004, p = 0.0001; t = 2.301, p
= 0.0214). **Results for all three parameter settings for staff time are
statistically significant** (t = 10.954, p = 0.0000; t = -4.527, p = 0.0000; t
= 3.058, p = 0.0023). When comparing the three parameter settings, we find
statistically significant differences for both execution time (Actual and Proposed
times, respectively: F = 17.4862, p = 0.0000; F = 425.464, p = 0.0000) and staff
time (F = 5.716, p = 0.0033; F = 206.488, p = 0.0000, respectively).

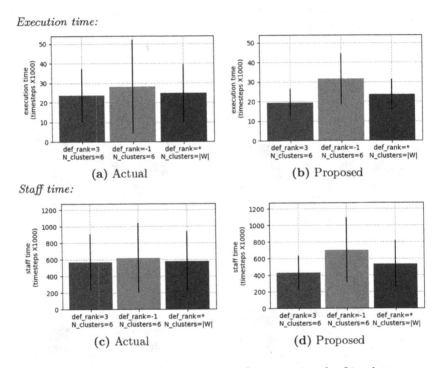

Fig. 3. Results for actual versus proposed teams using the *Live* data set.

However, for the two reasons described below, deciding which approach performs best is inconclusive. First, the default picking speed is inaccurate. As
shown in Fig. 3, for Proposed, there is a significant increase in time when the
default rank is decreased from 3 to −1; for Actual, the difference is not significant. The proposed teams contained more pickers assigned to fruits they had no
experience at picking than the actual teams. Thus, if the default rank (picking
speed) is set too high, it will inflate the difference between the proposed teams
and the actual teams. The inverse is also true: the default rank could be set too

low, causing the proposed teams to appear worse than they would actually be. Therefore, unless the default picking speed is not used, it is difficult to accurately evaluate results within simulation.

The second reason is due to inaccuracies in the estimated yield and the list of available workers. As mentioned in Sect. 4, the proposed teams (during the Live experiments) use the estimated yield and the worker availability lists since this is the information that will be available when the schedule is created. However, occasionally a field is estimated to be picked but is not actually picked, and vice versa. Therefore, the actual teams use the actual yield (since we do not have the deployed teams for fields that were not actually picked). This has resulted in the *(Live, Proposed)* experiment having a larger sample size than *(Live, Actual)*, as shown is Table 1. Further, some workers in the list of available workers may not actually work on certain days. Therefore, there will be differences in the resulting executing time and staff times caused by these inaccuracies.

6 Summary and Future Work

This paper has explored challenges affecting the evaluation and deployment of multi-agent task allocation methods for managing the harvesting workforce. Our results have shown that when using a historical data set, our proposed teams produced significantly shorter *staff time* than the actual teams. Although the parameter setting *(Def_rank = *, N_clusters = $|W|$)* produced the best staff time results for both actual and proposed teams, the result is not statistically significant. When using a live data set, our proposed teams produced significantly shorter *execution time* and *staff time* than actual teams with two of the three parameter settings, the best being *(Def_rank = 3, N_clusters = 6)*. There are still questions about the validity of our method, given the number of aspects that are difficult to reproduce in a simulation. For the upcoming season, we are planning an experiment with a commercial farm in which we deploy our proposed teams in order to evaluate our method in a more realistic way. This will also give us data through which we can improve our simulator.

In future work, we will investigate evaluating further parameter settings and task allocation mechanisms, trialing the proposed team allocations at a commercial farm and evaluating our approach on a hybrid robotic-human workforce.

Acknowledgments. This work was supported by Research England [Lincoln Agri-Robotics] as part of the Expanding Excellence in England (E3) Programme and by Ceres Agri-tech.

References

1. Chang, C.L., Lin, K.M.: Smart agricultural machine with a computer vision-based weeding and variable-rate irrigation scheme. Robotics **7**(3), 38 (2018)
2. Das, G., Cielniak, G., From, P., Hanheide, M.: Discrete event simulations for scalability analysis of robotic in-field logistics in agriculture-a case study. In: ICRA Workshop on Robotic Vision and Action in Agriculture (2018)

3. Dias, M.B., Zlot, R., Kalra, N., Stentz, A.: Market-based multirobot coordination: a survey and analysis. Proc. IEEE **94**(7), 1257–1270 (2006)
4. Duckett, T., Pearson, S., Blackmore, S., Grieve, B., Smith, M.: Agricultural robotics white paper: the future of robotic agriculture. https://www.ukras.org/wp-content/uploads/2018/10/UK_RAS_wp_Agri_web-res_single.pdf (2018)
5. Elkoby, Z., van 't Ooster, B., Edan, Y.: Simulation analysis of sweet pepper harvesting operations. In: Grabot, B., Vallespir, B., Gomes, S., Bouras, A., Kiritsis, D. (eds.) APMS 2014. IAICT, vol. 440, pp. 441–448. Springer, Heidelberg (2014). https://doi.org/10.1007/978-3-662-44733-8_55
6. Harman, H., Sklar, E.: Multi-agent task allocation for fruit picker team formation. In: Proceedings of the 21st International Conference on Autonomous Agents and Multiagent Systems (AAMAS) (2022)
7. Harman, H., Sklar, E.I.: A practical application of market-based mechanisms for allocating harvesting tasks. In: Dignum, F., Corchado, J.M., De La Prieta, F. (eds.) PAAMS 2021. LNCS (LNAI), vol. 12946, pp. 114–126. Springer, Cham (2021). https://doi.org/10.1007/978-3-030-85739-4_10
8. Heap, B., Pagnucco, M.: Repeated sequential single-cluster auctions with dynamic tasks for multi-robot task allocation with pickup and delivery. In: Klusch, M., Thimm, M., Paprzycki, M. (eds.) MATES 2013. LNCS (LNAI), vol. 8076, pp. 87–100. Springer, Heidelberg (2013). https://doi.org/10.1007/978-3-642-40776-5_10
9. Heap, B., Pagnucco, M.: Sequential single-cluster auctions for robot task allocation. In: Wang, D., Reynolds, M. (eds.) AI 2011. LNCS (LNAI), vol. 7106, pp. 412–421. Springer, Heidelberg (2011). https://doi.org/10.1007/978-3-642-25832-9_42
10. Kalra, N., Zlot, R., Dias, M.B., Stentz, A.: Market-based multirobot coordination: a comprehensive survey and analysis. Technical Reports CMU-RI-TR-05-16, Carnegie-Mellon University, Pittsburgh, USA (2005)
11. Kirk, R., Cielniak, G., Mangan, M.: L*a*b*fruits: a rapid and robust outdoor fruit detection system combining bio-inspired features with one-stage deep learning networks. Sensors **20**(1), 275 (2020)
12. Koenig, S., et al.: The power of sequential single-item auctions for agent coordination. In: Proceedings of AAAI, vol. 2 (2006)
13. Kootstra, G., Wang, X., Blok, P.M., Hemming, J., van Henten, E.: Selective harvesting robotics: current research, trends, and future directions. Curr. Robot. Rep. **2**(1), 95–104 (2021). https://doi.org/10.1007/s43154-020-00034-1
14. Kurtser, P., Edan, Y.: Planning the sequence of tasks for harvesting robots. Rob. Auton. Syst. **131**, 103591 (2020)
15. Liu, B., Bruch, R.: Weed detection for selective spraying: a review. Curr. Robot. Rep. **1**(1), 19–26 (2020). https://doi.org/10.1007/s43154-020-00001-w
16. Lujak, M., Sklar, E.I., Semet, F.: Agriculture fleet vehicle routing: a decentralised and dynamic problem. AI Commun. **34**(1), 1–17 (2021)
17. Luke, S., Cioffi-Revilla, C., Panait, L., Sullivan, K., Balan, G.: Mason: a multiagent simulation environment. SIMULATION **81**(7), 517–527 (2005)
18. Mitchell, T.M.: Machine Learning. McGraw-Hill, New York (1997)
19. Naik, G.: Global farming suffers from falling prices, labor shortages as virus spreads. S&P Global Market Intelligence (2020). https://www.spglobal.com/marketintelligence/en/news-insights/latest-news-headlines/global-farming-suffers-from-falling-prices-labor-shortages-as-virus-spreads-57836793
20. Partridge, J., Partington, R.: 'The anxiety is off the scale': UK farm sector worried by labour shortages. The Guardian (2021). https://www.theguardian.com/business/2021/aug/25/the-anxiety-is-off-the-scale-uk-farm-sector-worried-by-labour-shortages

21. Schneider, E., Sklar, E.I., Parsons, S.: Evaluating multi-robot teamwork in parameterised environments. In: Alboul, L., Damian, D., Aitken, J.M.M. (eds.) TAROS 2016. LNCS (LNAI), vol. 9716, pp. 301–313. Springer, Cham (2016). https://doi.org/10.1007/978-3-319-40379-3_32

22. Schneider, E., Sklar, E.I., Parsons, S., Özgelen, A.T.: Auction-based task allocation for multi-robot teams in dynamic environments. In: Dixon, C., Tuyls, K. (eds.) TAROS 2015. LNCS (LNAI), vol. 9287, pp. 246–257. Springer, Cham (2015). https://doi.org/10.1007/978-3-319-22416-9_29

23. Seyyedhasani, H., Peng, C., Jang, W.J., Vougioukas, S.G.: Collaboration of human pickers and crop-transporting robots during harvesting - part ii: simulator evaluation and robot-scheduling case-study. Comput. Electron. Agric. **172**, 105323 (2020)

24. Shamshiri, R.R., Hameed, I.A., Karkee, M., Weltzien, C.: Robotic harvesting of fruiting vegetables: a simulation approach in V-REP, ROS and MATLAB. In: Proceedings in Automation in Agriculture-Securing Food Supplies for Future Generations (2018)

25. Shapiro, S.S., Wilk, M.B.: An analysis of variance test for normality (complete samples). Biometrika **52**(3/4), 591–611 (1965)

Agents Dealing with Norms
and Regulations

Christian Kammler$^{(\boxtimes)}$, René Mellema , and Frank Dignum

Umeå Universitet, Umeå, Sweden
{christian.kammler,rene.mellema,frank.dignum}@umu.se

Abstract. Norms influence behaviour in many ways. In situations such as the COVID-19 pandemic where the effect of policies on the spread of the virus is evaluated, this leads to disputes about their effectiveness. In order to build agent-based social simulations that give proper support for this evaluation process we need agents that properly deal with norms. In this paper we present a new agent deliberation architecture that takes more aspects of norms into account than traditional architectures have done. Dealing properly with norms means that agents can reason through the consequences of the norms, that they are used to motivate and not just constrain behaviour, and that the agents can violate the norm as well. For the former we use the ideas of perspectives on norms, while the latter is enabled through the use of values. Within our architecture we can also represent habitual behaviour, context sensitive planning, and through the use of landmarks, reactive planning. We use the example of a restaurant-size based restriction to show how our architecture works.

Keywords: Social simulation · Normative reasoning · Values · Needs

1 Introduction

Norms influence behaviour in many ways, and on many different levels [7]. This makes it challenging for policy makers and other decision makers to create policies (which we see as special types of norms), as has been shown by the current COVID-19 pandemic. Here, heavy disputes arose on the effectiveness of the policies that had been introduced to combat the spread of the virus with regards to the effects that those policies had on the people. To tackle this, and to support policy and other decision makers, agent-based social simulation can be a powerful tool [13,15,17,24].

To build agent-based social simulations that give this support, the agents in the simulation need to show realistic human-like behaviour. Part of this is that they need to be able to properly reason with norms, i.e. seeing them as more than just restrictions on behavior. This requires not only that they can see if the consequences of following or breaking the norm are desirable for them, but also how they interact with other parts of their reasoning process. In particular, this means that norms cannot just be seen as simple restrictions, but we also need to

F. Lorig and E. Norling (Eds.): MABS 2022, LNAI 13743, pp. 134–146, 2023.
https://doi.org/10.1007/978-3-031-22947-3_11

take their motivational aspects into account [5,21]. Furthermore, a new policy often interacts with existing social structures (e.g. habits, social practices, other norms, goals) as well, which might cause them to change. Since norm breaking is an important part of norm dynamics [2, Chap. 5], the architecture will also need a flexible way to deal with norm violations that the other agents can react to. What this means for an architecture is that the norms cannot just be added as a module, but it has to be interwoven into the whole decision making process.

Therefore, we are presenting a deliberation architecture with social reasoning as its focus which is motivated by [10]. To enable agents to reason through the consequences of the norms, we use the concept of perspectives on norms that we introduced in [17]. We thereby also take the motivational aspects of norms into account, and enable agents to reason about norm violations. Within our architecture we use context sensitive planning, so agents can adjust their goals and plans reactively with the help of landmarks, based on their current context. Having context sensitive planning also allows us to model habitual behaviour by enabling the agents to recognise whether they are in a familiar context.

While there has been work on norms in the agent community, including work on norm violation behaviour, such as [3,6,7,10,21,26], they do not address all the requirements for properly dealing with norms. Problems with architectures [3,21] for example are that norms are only seen as obligations, and not motivations. Furthermore, they are not allowing an agent to reason "consciously" about a specific norm to determine by themselves if they want to violate the norm or not.

2   Elements of a Normative Agent Architecture

To have an agent architecture which allows agents to take the motivational aspects of norms into account, as well as being able to reason "consciously" about breaking a norm, we need a variety of elements which we are going to describe in more detail in this section.

With these elements we can then also take norms into account which are active later in the day in a different context. For example: Going to a bar in the evening after work with colleagues (norm) means that we might leave the car at home in the morning, so we do not drink and drive (norm, i.e. not violating the no alcohol when driving norm).

Such ahead planning is very complex for an agent compared to humans. For us it is obvious and thought of as one thing, but for agents it is comprised of multiple things where each step of the day requires new deliberation of the agent. To enable agents to have more of this long-term planning, we are using the concepts of context and plan patterns in our architecture.

We first talk about how we use norms in more detail, and then talk about the different elements concerning the agent itself.

2.1   Norms

Norms describe 'normal' behavior and aim at assuring the interests and values of groups or the society as a whole [19]. Furthermore, they are not only constraints on behavior. They can also motivate [5,21] and trigger new behavior [19]. Also, norms promote and demote values. This makes it possible for agents to deliberate if the norm is important for them or if they want to violate it. We take the idea that norms promote values from the real world, as norms are created with a purpose. For example: The norm to wear a face mask is created to reduce the spread of the coronavirus and thus, promotes safety.

To formulate norms, we use our ADICDlRO framework [17]. The elements in the ADICDlRO framework are as follows.

A defines the agent group that the norm is applicable for.

D is the deontic part of the norm, and together with the aim (I), they form the {fulfilment, violation} condition of the norm.

C defines the contexts in which the norm is active and not active, therefore representing the {activation, deactivation} condition of the norm.

The deadline element (Dl) states when the norm is supposed to be fulfilled.

The repair part (R) of the framework defines the action(s) to 'undo' the potential breaking of the norm, and the 'Or else' (O) specifies the punishment of the norm violation.

2.2   Needs

Needs are motivators that drive us constantly to perform behaviour that satisfies them. We make use of this in our architecture in the form of *long-term goals*. Long-term goals are abstract in nature and can be seen as the root element of a goal-plan tree or a goal-goal tree. They have a variety of sub-goals which we call *short-term goals*, which present steps towards fulfilling the long-term goal. We assume that the long-term goals are never achieved. They are ideals that can be seen as points on a horizon, but have no concrete state that can be true or false. A way to implement this is using a homeostatic model, see e.g. [10,14]. The needs are represented as containers in the architecture that deplete over time, and can be filled by achieving subgoals related to the specific long-term goal. The priority in values (see next section) determines thereby the urgency to satisfy the need for taking steps towards a certain long-term goal.

Furthermore, they are a fixed, pre-determined set in our architecture. To determine them, we can, for example, ask the stakeholders that are represented in the specific model.

2.3   Goals and Values

Values are used to evaluate behaviour and events [17,19,21], and function as standards for the evaluation criteria [23,25]. We use values in the architecture to determine which goals are important to achieve, which actions are most desirable to take to achieve the goals, and which needs are more urgent to satisfy. Each perspective has its own priority of values [17] which are constant over time during the whole simulation.

Goals are states that the agent wants to achieve. Goals in our architecture are, called *short-term goals*. These are representing steps towards the desired long-term goals of the agent, and are generated in the goal generation step in our architecture, and can be seen as child nodes in a goal-plan tree or a goal-goal tree.

The formation of these short-term goals is influenced by the agent's priorities in values. The norms influence the short-term goals in the way that some goals might be forbidden due to a prohibition, or an obligation is in conflict with the goal, and therefore achieving the goal will be in violation of the obligation, over which the agent can deliberate.

To achieve a goal, specific actions are taken by the agent. This can be done by one action or a sequence of actions might be necessary to achieve the goal. When the goal is reached, the associated needs will be satisfied and connected values will be promoted and demoted. Note here, that a short-term goal (StG) can be associated with more that one need, i.e. it is contributing to more than one long-term goal. Previously generated short-term goals can be used in the same context again.

2.4 Perspectives

People use their own motivations and have different goals, plans and capabilities. Therefore, we are using the concept of *perspectives* [17] to connect norms to individual behavior. Thus agents only focus on the parts of the norm which are relevant for them, and only those parts are affecting their behaviour, utilising the ADICDIRO framework of norms [17]. To address this, perspectives have the following elements [17, p. 142]: "A perspective is specified by goals (G), available actions (A), effects of those actions (EoA), social affordances (SocAffs), and priorities in values (PrioV)."

The *PrioV* determines which kind of behaviour is important to us and which incentives motivate us the most. In terms of goal selection and formation, they also help us to select the goals which are most desirable for us whereby goals are specific to a perspective, as everyone has specific goals in their minds which fits their needs. Furthermore, we are distinguishing two kinds of actions, the (classical) physical actions, and social actions. Social actions are the social effects of the physical action performed which are the *SocAffs* in our definition. Note that $SocAffs \neq EoA$ as EoA are the physical effects of the action A, and *SocAffs* the social effects of the physical action, i.e. the social action.

2.5 Actions

To achieve the goals, and satisfy the needs, the agent has a set of available actions. We differentiate hereby between physical actions and social actions [17].

Physical actions are the classical actions when we think of actions. They may require one or more objects (o_i, o_j, ...), with $o_i, o_j \in O$, to perform the action, whereby O is the total set of n objects $O = \{o_1, ..., o_n\}$ that we have in our simulation. Actions also have a pre-condition that needs to be met so the action can be executed. The actions also have an effect, the result of the action [17]. Furthermore, they are specific to a perspective, as different groups have different actions available to them.

Social actions are defined by the social effects of the physical actions (including all physical actions that the agent can perform= performed [17]. They call this the *"social affordances (SocAffs) of an object* (o_i)*"* [17, p. 6]. In general, we relate them to the purpose that an object fulfils for a person or a group [8]. People have different purposes for the same object based on their perspective.

Norms influence actions in the way that some actions might become obligatory or forbidden. Identifying the actions that are affected by a norm is done using the object of the norm (I_{Object}), by checking if $o_i == I_{Object}$ holds, where o_i is the object required by the action. We note that we assume here that an action always requires an object.

Finally, actions promote and demote values. We note here however, that a sequence of actions to achieve a goal can promote and demote different values in the end than the individual actions in that chain. This happens because achieving goals can also promote and demote values.

2.6 Context

Keeping all the different goals, actions, and norms in mind, greatly increase the complexity of the decision making process. To constrain this, we use the notion of *context* [28], which contains all the information that is currently *relevant* [4]. For example, this can mean that the currently active norms are part of the context, but the ones that are currently deactivated need not be. Thereby making the deliberation faster for the agent since it needs to take less things into account. Furthermore, keeping track of the context also helps in detecting when the goal might no longer be achievable.

To determine what information is relevant, we base ourselves on the work of [4,27]. Here, relevancy of information is defined in terms of the *goal* that the agent has. This means that the context should contain information that:

1. is about the content (proposition) of the goal;
2. is about the relationships between the goals;
3. is about the conditions for the pertinent actions.

What exactly this information is depends on the exact simulation, but there are some general rules for this. Firstly, the goal itself is included. At least the active norms are incorporated based on their active contexts (C), since they can allow or block certain actions. To further determine what information is relevant, we check which information is needed to execute the current plan. This would also be a good place to bring in expert knowledge. If we know which plans and actions are available, and we know which information these need to determine their pre-conditions, we can use this to determine what information is relevant towards the goal.

To determine whether the agent has to switch contexts, we can set up *acceptable* ranges for the parameters. This can be done using a similar process as determining which parameters are relevant, but now keeping in mind not just what parameters are relevant, but also the values that they need to have. Then in order to check if we are still in the same context, we can compare the current value of the relevant parameters to these ranges. Once a parameter has left that range, the context has changed too much, and the agent has to replan or change their goal entirely.

To make it easier to talk about the context, and to link actions and plans to specific contexts, we *label* contexts. Actions/plans are linked to these context labels instead of having to be linked to more detailed context descriptions.

Using the goal as the cornerstone in the context detection, does mean that we are making the assumption that there will always be a goal. This might not be the case when a goal has just been achieved. In this case, we assume that there is a default context that defines the relevant information. This should include at least its current needs, the roles the agent fulfils, and the time/location.

2.7 Plan Patterns

When designing agent behaviour, there is often a balance that needs to be made between proactive, goal directed behaviour, and reactive situational behaviour. Our solution to this problem is through the use of plan patterns [8]. Plan patterns are sets of sequences of actions, defined in terms of *landmarks* [11]. Landmarks represent states that need to be achieved along the way, without specifying how they are achieved. In this way, they can be seen as sub-goals in a plan, but achieving them does not have the same effect that achieving a goal has. Using this system, the agents can make a rough plan to follow, and then fill in the details depending on the current context.

This requires some changes to the traditional planning paradigm. Instead of giving full fledged plan, the planner now needs to produce plan patterns instead. As long as there is a mechanism for chaining landmarks together, this is not a big change. The context can also help here in speeding things up, since within a certain context, only certain landmarks might be available. Since we are trying to mimic human behaviour, which is often repetitive (i.e. habitual) but not always optimal, we can also store plan patterns that were used before in the same context. Thereby giving us the possibility to simulate habitual behaviour.

After a plan pattern has been selected, the landmarks need to be filled in. To do this, a lower level plan is selected, where the plan can be just one action. This is done in a similar manner as the selection of an initial plan, but now the landmark is what is being planned towards instead of the goal. Here again the context, which might be slightly different from the context when the initial plan was made, can be used to limit or make available certain options in the planning.

To account for desired actions becoming not executable anymore during plan execution, we mark actions with a *purpose* for why they have been selected. With this, the agent can find an alternative action or plan pattern that serves the same purpose. To avoid the alternative action/plan becoming too long, we limit its length before forcing the agent to create a new plan to reach the goal.

2.8 Norm Breaking

So far we have discussed norms and described the different mechanisms we need to deal with the different sources of motivations. To decide between these different sources, we use the notion of plan/action *acceptability*.

Acceptability here means that for each plan/action selected by the agent which is in conflict with a norm, the agent needs to find executing the plan/action acceptable with respect to breaking the norm. We use values for this decision. Since each norm pro-/demotes different values, the agent can compare what values it deems important with those. If the norm demotes values it finds important, then it should break the norm. Other indicators can also be taken into account, such as governmental trust (in the case of legal norms) or its social identity.

If the agent does not find the norm acceptable to break, then it tries to find an alternative plan/action. This can also happen if a norm applies that it had not anticipated would be active, in which case it would end up in the "find alternative action" step. If no alternative is available, the agent tries to generate a new plan in the "planner" to achieve the goal. If that also fails, the agent marks the goal as not achievable, and generates a new goal.

However, if it does find the norm acceptable to break, then it can break the norm. In that case, the norm violation would have to be detected by the software, and in the next time step, both the reparation (R) and 'or else' (O) parts of the norm have to be activated as well.

2.9 Resulting Agent Architecture

Putting the things together from the previous sections, we get the architecture in Fig. 1. The starting point of the deliberation is the *context detection*, and the end point is the *execute action*. The solid arrows indicate the next step, and the dotted arrows of needs, values, and norms are indicating the influence of those elements.

To show how our architecture works in practice, we use a restriction on the number of allowed guests based on the size of the restaurant, similar to our last paper [17]. Given the current COVID-19 pandemic, only a certain amount of guests are allowed inside a restaurant to increase the distance between the guests in the restaurant to promote the value safety. Looking at this norm only as a restriction is not enough and only leads to the trivial insight that the restaurant has too little income and is eventually going bankrupt, because not enough guests are allowed in the restaurant. This view is too limited, as different people are in different ways, such as the guests and the restaurant owner.

Making money with their restaurant is the most important need for **restaurant owner**, given their highest prioritised values are power and achievement. At their restaurant they get informed about the new norm (context detection).

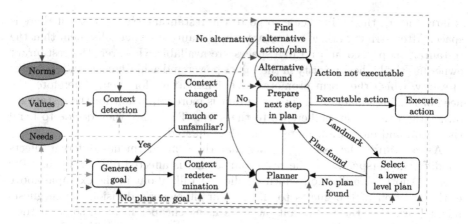

Fig. 1. The resulting agent architecture

The new norm hinders the restaurant owner to have as many guests as possible in their restaurant (goal), and therefore negatively impacts the need of making money with the restaurant. Consequently, the context changed too much for the restaurant owner. Given a high priority in the values of power and achievement, it is very important for the restaurant owner to make as much money as possible with their restaurant. Therefore, they are now looking for a way (generate goal) to combat the loss of income which is a consequence of the new norm. The restaurant owner decides to lower their variable costs of the restaurant (new goal), given their priority in power and achievement. To achieve this goal, the restaurant owner determines their new context (which contains information about food prices, contracts with suppliers and staff, norms such as minimum wage or which meat is allowed in food), and forms the plan (in the planner) to use cheaper ingredients in some of their meat dishes. The next step in the plan is a landmark (collecting all information about the meat dishes served in the restaurant), so the restaurant owner selects a lower level plan with all the dishes in menu order. They decide to use cheaper meat in the dishes where a lot of sauce and spices are used (such as goulash), because there guests will not taste the change as much.

While for many non regular restaurant **guests**, the norm of limiting the amount of guests in a restaurant affects their behaviour strongly and they might decide to reserve a table before hand (similar deliberation as the restaurant owner), for some of the regular guests the norm does not change their context too much. Consider a group of friends who goes to the same restaurant every Friday after work. They have their specific table reserved every week. Therefore, the introduction of the new norm does not change their context too much for them. However, this time their desired beer is not available due to shortages. Therefore, they decide to have a different beer (find alternative action) with a similar taste. In another instance, a new colleague decides to join their regular table. While this changes the context too much for the group (given a new person is introduced), they still decide to go to the restaurant trying to see if there is space. After arriving at the restaurant, the restaurant owner tells them that the restaurant is packed and no free spaces are available. However, the restaurant owner has the highest priority in the values power and achievement, and the value of safety, which the norm promotes, is not important for them. Therefore, the need of making money with the restaurant is more important for the restaurant owner than the strong adherence to the norm. Therefore, they decide to bend the norm, and have a few more guests than allowed.

As a result, the example shows that the same norm has different effects for different perspectives. The restaurant owner is affected differently than the guests. Another implication which we did not talk about in the example above is the reaction of the guests to the restaurant owner's decision. Some guests might learn that the restaurant owner is using cheaper meat in some of their dishes. This might not change the context for some guests, as they do not eat the affected dishes. However, for the people who eat those dishes it changes the context too much. Also here, for some guests it might not be as important as the restaurant place itself, as sustainability is not so important to them compared to the eating place. However, for guests for whom sustainability has a very high or the highest priority, they are not going to that restaurant anymore. Therefore, modelling norms as just a restriction on behaviour is not adequate to model all the consequences of the introduction of a new regulation or norm.

3   Related Work

Having shown our architecture, we can now discuss why existing approaches, such as the ones mentioned in the introduction are not suitable for our purposes.

3.1   BDI, its Extensions and Utility Functions

One of the big downsides of using BDI [22] and its extensions, such as [3,20], is that they tend to not take into account the full agent deliberation cycle, in particular norm importance in planning. Besides this, they also tend to not take into account the context that an agent is in and how that interacts with decision making, nor other motivational reasons for norm following/breaking besides the agents desires/intentions.

While there are works that address the first concern, such as [21], these tend to not address the reasons why an agent might want to break or follow a norm. As described in Chap. 11 in [2], agents might have various different reasons for breaking norms, not all of which are depent on their other desires or intentions, but sometimes simply how much they like the norm, or who instituted it. Specifying when and how an agent should find breaking a norm "acceptable" in a BDI framework has to our knowledge not yet happened.

The context problem is easiest seen with BOID [3]. In the BOID architecture, agents are of a certain type to solve conflicts between different types of motivations, such as obligations and desires. This type does not differ over the lifetime of the agent. However, in real life a lot of the decisions that we make are dependent upon the context in which we make them, which includes our reasons for breaking or following a norm [2]. These kinds of factors are hard to include in the BOID architecture, but are accounted for in our proposal.

Approaches based on utilities (including sanctions and rewards), such as [20] or the EMIL-A architecture by [6] with its EMIL-I-A [26] extension, solve some of these issues, but it still has a few drawbacks as pointed out by [12]. Usually, a utility function is conceptualised in such a way that norm breaking behaviour results in utility penalties [12]. Furthermore, these functions only function well in a static environment [9]. Furthermore, given the same set of alternatives, the choice is always the same [9], even though the context might have changed.

3.2   Social Reasoning

[10] in their ASSOCC project shows the benefits of having an architecture that is capable of social reasoning. The results of their COVID-19 simulations seem to be far more close to actual human behavior than most other approaches. At the core of the agent's decision making process is a homeostatic needs model, which is described in detail in [16].

Each of the agents has several needs, which are modelled as containers (based on [14]). These containers deplete over time if no action towards satisfying that need is taken [16]. The actions can also cause the draining of the container by removing some satisfaction. An action can thus influence multiple needs at the same time. For example, going to a park with friends satisfies the need of belonging, as one is with their friends. However, in the COVID crisis it also has a negative impact on risk-avoidance, as one is outside around people [16]. The decision which action to take next is made based on the combined need satisfaction over all needs that the action would provide, if executed.

A major issue which makes the ASSOCC architecture not usable for our purposes is that norms are only modelled implicitly, in their effect on the need satisfaction of an action. This makes changing the norms very difficult, as each of the parts of the model has to be inspected to see if this part of the code is affected by the desired change. Furthermore, this also means that the agents cannot reason about the norms themselves when determining whether they should violate them. These aspects make it is not suitable for our more general architecture.

4   Discussion

Our architecture provides a deliberation that can be very fast and simple when plan (patterns) are available for the current context, i.e. mimiking habitual behavior (the middle line from context detection to action execution in Fig. 1. The contextual planning involving values, goals and norms is only used if no ready plan is available. This makes the agent very efficient in all standard situations, while taking all the social aspects into consideration when it is needed.

It is clear that agents with different perspectives react on different aspects of norms. Thus, modelling norms as just a restriction on behaviour would not be adequate to model all the consequences of the introduction of a new norm. We showed this in our example discussion of the architecture even if different groups share the same values (in our case sustainability).

Since our framework allows for norm violation, there are also multiple directions for future work in this area. The first of these is that our notion of "acceptable plan" can be expanded. For example, most norms are put in place by some form of institution, either a formal institute such as a state, or an informal one such as a culture. One thing that could be taken into account is how much an agent might trust such an institution, since this also has a large effect in human societies [18]. Another aspect which we did not discuss in the example is the reaction of the guests to the norm violation of the restaurant owner (having a few more guests than allowed). While for some guests this does not matter, others might leave, because they feel that their safety is endangered.

Norm internalisation [1], which is an important aspect of normative reasoning, also needs to be explored. A norm that is internalised is harder to violate than a norm that is not internalised. In general a norm can be said to be internalised if the norm is in line with the agents values. Thus an agent would choose the behaviour that follows the norm even if that norm would not be there. Having the norm has more effects as we have seen, and thus, the norm is an important driver of behaviour.

For our immediate future work, we are going to implement our proposed architecture, based on the formalisation which we omitted in this paper to not distract from the main goal of the paper to present an agent architecture capable of incorporating different perspectives on norms, the motivation components of norms, and enabling agents to explicitly reason about norm violations.

References

1. Axelrod, R.: An evolutionary approach to norms. Am. Polit. Sci. Rev. **80**(04), 1095–1111 (1986). https://doi.org/10.2307/1960858
2. Brennan, G., Eriksson, L., Goodin, R.E., Southwood, N.: Explaining Norms. Oxford University Press, Oxford (2013)
3. Broersen, J., Dastani, M., Hulstijn, J., Huang, Z., van der Torre, L.: The BOID architecture: conflicts between beliefs, obligations, intentions and desires. In: Proceedings of the Fifth International Conference on Autonomous Agents, pp. 9–16. Association for Computing Machinery, New York (2001)
4. Castelfranchi, C.: Guarantees for autonomy in cognitive agent architecture. In: Wooldridge, M.J., Jennings, N.R. (eds.) ATAL 1994. LNCS, vol. 890, pp. 56–70. Springer, Heidelberg (1995). https://doi.org/10.1007/3-540-58855-8_3
5. Castelfranchi, C., Dignum, F., Jonker, C.M., Treur, J.: Deliberative normative agents: principles and architecture. In: Jennings, N.R., Lespérance, Y. (eds.) ATAL 1999. LNCS (LNAI), vol. 1757, pp. 364–378. Springer, Heidelberg (2000). https://doi.org/10.1007/10719619_27

6. Conte, R., Andrighetto, G., Campennl, M.: Minding Norms: Mechanisms and Dynamics of Social Order in Agent Societies. Oxford University Press, New York (2014)
7. Dignum, F.: Autonomous agents with norms. Artif. Intell. Law **7**, 69–79 (1999). https://doi.org/10.1023/A:1008315530323
8. Dignum, F.: Interactions as social practices: towards a formalization. arXiv preprint arXiv:1809.08751 (2018)
9. Dignum, F.: Foundations of social simulations for crisis situations. In: Dignum, F. (ed.) Social Simulation for a Crisis. CSS, pp. 15–37. Springer, Cham (2021). https://doi.org/10.1007/978-3-030-76397-8_2
10. Dignum, F. (ed.): Social Simulation for a Crisis. CSS, Springer, Cham (2021). https://doi.org/10.1007/978-3-030-76397-8
11. Dignum, V., Dignum, F.: Coordinating tasks in agent organizations. In: Noriega, P., et al. (eds.) COIN -2006. LNCS (LNAI), vol. 4386, pp. 32–47. Springer, Heidelberg (2007). https://doi.org/10.1007/978-3-540-74459-7_3
12. Fagundes, M.S., Ossowski, S., Cerquides, J., Noriega, P.: Design and evaluation of norm-aware agents based on normative Markov decision processes. Int. J. Approx. Reason. **78**, 33–61 (2016)
13. Gilbert, N., Ahrweiler, P., Barbrook-Johnson, P., Narasimhan, K.P., Wilkinson, H.: Computational modelling of public policy: reflections on practice. J. Artif. Soc. Soc. Simul. **21**(1), 14 (2018). https://doi.org/10.18564/jasss.3669
14. Heidari, S., Jensen, M., Dignum, F.: Simulations with values. In: Verhagen, H., Borit, M., Bravo, G., Wijermans, N. (eds.) Advances in Social Simulation. SPC, pp. 201–215. Springer, Cham (2020). https://doi.org/10.1007/978-3-030-34127-5_19
15. Jager, W., van der Vegt, G.: Management of complex systems: toward agent-based gaming for policy. In: Janssen, M., Wimmer, M.A., Deljoo, A. (eds.) Policy Practice and Digital Science. PAIT, vol. 10, pp. 291–303. Springer, Cham (2015). https://doi.org/10.1007/978-3-319-12784-2_13
16. Jensen, M., Vanhée, L., Kammler, C.: Social simulations for crises: from theories to implementation. In: Dignum, F. (ed.) Social Simulation for a Crisis. CSS, pp. 39–84. Springer, Cham (2021). https://doi.org/10.1007/978-3-030-76397-8_3
17. Kammler, C., Dignum, F., Wijermans, N., Lindgren, H.: Changing perspectives: adaptable interpretations of norms for agents. In: Van Dam, K.H., Verstaevel, N. (eds.) MABS 2021. LNCS (LNAI), vol. 13128, pp. 139–152. Springer, Cham (2022). https://doi.org/10.1007/978-3-030-94548-0_11
18. Marien, S., Hooghe, M.: Does political trust matter? An empirical investigation into the relation between political trust and support for law compliance. Eur. J. Political Res. **50**(2), 267–291 (2011)
19. Mellema, R., Jensen, M., Dignum, F.: Social rules for agent systems. In: Aler Tubella, A., Cranefield, S., Frantz, C., Meneguzzi, F., Vasconcelos, W. (eds.) COIN/COINE 2017/2020. LNCS (LNAI), vol. 12298, pp. 175–180. Springer, Cham (2021). https://doi.org/10.1007/978-3-030-72376-7_10
20. Meneguzzi, F., Rodrigues, O., Oren, N., Vasconcelos, W.W., Luck, M.: BDI reasoning with normative considerations. Eng. Appl. Artif. Intell. **43**, 127–146 (2015)
21. Panagiotidi, S., Alvarez-Napagao, S., Vázquez-Salceda, J.: Towards the norm-aware agent: bridging the gap between deontic specifications and practical mechanisms for norm monitoring and norm-aware planning. In: Balke, T., Dignum, F., van Riemsdijk, M.B., Chopra, A.K. (eds.) COIN 2013. LNCS (LNAI), vol. 8386, pp. 346–363. Springer, Cham (2014). https://doi.org/10.1007/978-3-319-07314-9_19

22. Rao, A.S., Georgeff, M.P., et al.: BDI agents: from theory to practice. In: Lesser, V., Gasser, L. (eds.) Proceedings of the First International Conference on Multiagent Systems, vol. 95, pp. 312–319. MIT Press, Cambridge (1995)
23. Rohan, M.J.: A rose by any name? The values construct. Pers. Soc. Psychol. Rev. **4**(3), 255–277 (2000)
24. Rosewell, B.: Complexity science and the art of policy making. In: Johnson, J., Nowak, A., Ormerod, P., Rosewell, B., Zhang, Y.-C. (eds.) Non-Equilibrium Social Science and Policy. UCS, pp. 159–178. Springer, Cham (2017). https://doi.org/10.1007/978-3-319-42424-8_11
25. Schwartz, S.H., Bilsky, W.: Toward a universal psychological structure of human values. J. Pers. Soc. Psychol. **53**(3), 550 (1987)
26. Segura, D.V.: Social norms for self-policing multiagent systems and virtual societies. Universitat Autonoma de Barcelona (2012)
27. Vecht, B.V.D.: Adjustable autonomy: controling influences on decision making. Universiteit Utrecht, Utrecht (2009)
28. Zimmermann, A., Lorenz, A., Oppermann, R.: An operational definition of context. In: Kokinov, B., Richardson, D.C., Roth-Berghofer, T.R., Vieu, L. (eds.) CONTEXT 2007. LNCS (LNAI), vol. 4635, pp. 558–571. Springer, Heidelberg (2007). https://doi.org/10.1007/978-3-540-74255-5_42

Author Index

Printed in the United States
by Baker & Taylor Publisher Services